Inasmuch

Christian Social Responsibility
in the Twentieth Century

*And the King shall answer and say unto them, Verily I say unto
you, Inasmuch as ye have done it unto one of the least of these
my brethren, ye have done it unto me* (Matthew 25:40).

Inasmuch

Christian Social Responsibility
in the Twentieth Century

David O. Moberg
Oct. 13, 1987

by

DAVID O. MOBERG

Bethel College and Seminary
St. Paul, Minnesota

WILLIAM B. EERDMANS PUBLISHING COMPANY
GRAND RAPIDS, MICHIGAN

ISBN 0-8028-1134-5

First printing, June 1965
Second printing, January 1968
Third printing, May 1970
Fourth printing, November 1973

Preface

My five years of service as chairman of the social agency and welfare committee of my denomination convinced me of the need for guidelines to direct the social welfare activities of evangelical churches. Without them, these activities can only result in a fragmentary program that haphazardly pursues many different problems and perhaps leaves the most important untouched. The proliferation of agencies and projects in the absence of an over-all philosophy and strategy is likely to result in self-contradictions in the total program. It also may cause unwholesome competition for funds, personnel, and other support among agencies that ought to work together. Programs thus may be extended in a manner that is inconsistent with the realities of the contemporary world and out of harmony with the organizational structure and administrative policies of supporting denominations.

Our committee therefore turned its attention to developing a Christian philosophy of social concern. I prepared a working paper which the committee subsequently recommended for revision and publication in book form. The paper then was circulated to a large number of pastors, professors, and people in welfare-related positions, nearly fifty of whom enthusiastically sent comments for its improvement. A pastor of a large Chicago church, for example, wrote that the statement was

> informative, inspirational, and, I must admit, incriminating. All ministers, I am sure, recognize that we have not given sufficient time to community-wide social needs. . . . the Church needs to recognize that a minister engaged in community welfare is in fact engaged in Christian work. Too often our concern in the matters of suffering is limited and circumscribed to church members only. . . . compassion must go beyond the limits of the church. It must extend into the community in areas which may never bring visible results to the local church.

5

Another pastor indicated that discussion periods with a group of teenagers in vacation Bible school the previous summer had convinced him that the church must give serious attention to current social issues. If it does not, youth will "lose their interest in Christ and His church — and thereby [we will] unknowingly be active agents in leading them astray!"

This book is intended as a starting point for study, thought, discussion, prayer, and work on the subject of Christian social responsibility. I hope it will stimulate effective action on matters related to the church's mission to society.

I have attempted to maintain a consistently evangelical Protestant orientation. Some readers may wonder why certain of the recommended readings come from theologically liberal sources. The main reason is simply that most work on Christian social concern has been done by the liberals.

I make no apology for recommending these readings. All Protestants share a common commitment to Jesus Christ and to the Bible as their guide to faith and conduct. They may disagree with one another about many details, but they all can learn from each other. I do not endorse all the references completely, but they have stimulated my thinking and will give many ideas to the intelligent reader.

My ideas, as well as those of the references recommended, should be subjected to critical analysis. Like the Bereans of old (Acts 17:11), the noble Christian of today searches the Scriptures daily to see whether the words of his contemporaries are in accord with the supreme guidebook.

The Bible references frequently inserted are not intended as "proof texts." Rather, they are listed to identify the location of passages and phrases cited or quoted. Some provide a starting point for topical Bible study. Others illustrate a new point with familiar concepts. In many instances they summarize briefly the teaching of the Scriptures on the respective subjects.

All Bible quotations are from the Authorized or King James Version, which is the most widely used translation among evangelicals. I encourage readers, however, to compare several modern translations of these passages, since contemporary wording often makes God's Word sharply relevant at points that previously were obscured by overfamiliar or archaic language.

This book provides a general philosophy of Christian social

responsibility. It is not a detailed handbook for dealing with specific social problems, nor is it strictly a social science treatise, though I trust that it is based soundly upon social science knowledge as well as upon Christian teachings.

Inasmuch is designed for interested pastors and laymen. Its ten chapters should make it easy to use in leadership training courses, discussion groups, and young people's and adult classes in Sunday school. I hope it will also be useful as collateral reading for students who wish to relate Christian values to their college courses on social problems, social science, social welfare, and ethics. Theological seminary students taking courses on social ethics, the church and society, and practical theology will also find it helpful.

I am grateful to the four dozen persons who read my committee paper on "A Christian Philosophy of Social Concern" and sent me their comments. Their suggestions have all received careful attention, even though not all have been fully implemented. Dr. Virgil Olson, Professor of Church History in Bethel Theological Seminary, contributed many of the ideas incorporated into Chapter 2. Miss Jean Lindblom, Bethel College's Faculty Secretary, graciously and efficiently typed the manuscript. My gratitude for indirect but important assistance is due also to many teachers, friends, and pastors, including first of all my own father, who during my most formative years was almost the only preacher I heard.

Participant observation as an American citizen, experiences as a Protestant church member, officer, lay preacher, and student pastor, books and articles on social ethics, and studies in the sociology of religion have all helped to shape the ideas expressed here. There is nothing new in this book except its organization. I have nothing that I did not receive from others. To my Sovereign Lord, as well as to all who have been used by Him, I extend my thanks for the valid insights and a plea for forgiveness for my mistakes.

DAVID O. MOBERG

St. Paul, Minnesota

Contents

PART I:
INTRODUCTION

Chapter 1

The Social Responsibility of the Christian

*I pray not that thou shouldest take them out of the world,
but that thou shouldest keep them from the evil. . . . As thou
hast sent me into the world, even so have I also sent them
into the world* (John 17:15, 18).

EVERY CHRISTIAN AND EVERY CHRISTIAN CHURCH IS INVOLVED IN
society and its problems. There are no exceptions. Even the
pastor, congregation, or denomination that claims to be ministering to purely spiritual needs is thereby declaring its position
on the political, economic, and social issues of its community
and nation.

This is true because the spiritual life of any person is profoundly social, no matter how "individualistic" or private it seems
to be. Its origin is social, for faith comes by hearing, and human
messengers are used by God to bring the gospel message
(Rom. 10:14-17). Even when a person is "alone with God,"
his emotions, sentiments, private prayers, conscience, language,
religious concepts, beliefs, values, and attitudes toward himself,
the world, and God are all modified by his past experiences in
society.

When a person worships with other people, he is in a social
situation which is shaped by the language, laws, and customs
of the surrounding political community and cultural group.
Society establishes patterns of relationships and rules for activities
which must be observed by churches under penalty of law.
Current problems of some churches in regard to zoning ordinances, building codes, health regulations, legal restrictions on

13

broadcasting, decrees about tract distribution and rules for street meetings reflect the social involvement of organized religion. Whenever a religious group is organized (and organization is evident in even the most informal groups if they have any sort of order whatever), it is a social unit. It typically reflects the patterns which are common in its society.

Religion is never "purely personal." It always is social as well. It is never limited to communication and interaction with God alone; it always involves social relationships with men as well. Even the most "mystical" of personal religious experiences has social overtones and effects.

Neutrality Is Impossible

Christians who attempt to be neutral toward the social issues of their day in effect are saying at least two significant things. Their action implies, first, that their spiritual message is totally irrelevant to practical problems except, perhaps, as it might change the motivations and aspirations of individuals who respond to it. They thus deny implicitly the direct, literal statements of hundreds of passages in the Bible which imply or specifically state that Christians must be actively concerned about social problems and other societal issues.

Second, the attempt to be neutral through a policy of inaction also conveys, implicitly, an endorsement of the status quo. It puts one into the position of seeming to bless or sanctify evil leaders, institutions, and practices instead of exposing and condemning the works of darkness. Christians above all others ought not to be conformed to this world (Rom. 12:2). Neither ought they to participate in the unfruitful works of darkness; instead they should expose them, walking as children of light (Eph. 5:7-17). Approval of the status quo usually is the equivalent of approving the vested interests of power and wealth, implying that such persons and organizations are always morally right in social controversies.

For such reasons, "no position" really *is* a position. No person or group in modern democratic society avoids social involvement.

A true concern for individual persons necessitates a concern for these same people as members of large-scale organizations and participants in widely diffused institutions like government, busi-

14

ness, industry, education, social welfare, mass communications, science, and technology. Every person functions as businessman or laborer, producer or consumer, buyer or seller, teacher or pupil, parent or child, and in numerous other social roles. Christians, therefore, cannot be neutral on social issues because their neighbors, whom they are to love, are social beings.

If a church's members and especially its leaders are not aware of this inevitable involvement with "worldly affairs" and "society outside the church," it can drift aimlessly with the ebb and flow of circumstance. As a result, it might eventually change into an organization whose programs actually contradict its own teachings. It may even violate basic doctrines of Scripture, which it claims as its sole guide to faith and conduct.

An honest recognition of the social involvement of every Christian and every church can therefore help to prevent heretical doctrines and misguided practices.

The Call to Social Action

Christian responsibility for social needs is expressed in numerous Scripture passages. Even the Great Commission with its stress upon going into *all* the world and "teaching them to observe all things whatsoever I have commanded you" (Matt. 28:20) carries an indirect commandment for active social concern as well as for conventional programs of evangelism and missions.

Many evangelical spokesmen have called for a renewed emphasis upon the social obligations of the Christian. Carl F. H. Henry noted that the redemptive gospel once was a world-changing message, but that it had been narrowed to a world-resisting message by an embarrassing divorce between individual salvation and community responsibility. He called for a "new reformation" which would make clear the implications of divinely given personal regeneration for individual and social problems.[1]

This call for a renewed concern with social problems was repeated by the Rev. E. Edwin Paulson in the official magazine of the National Association of Evangelicals:

[1] *The Uneasy Conscience of Modern Fundamentalism* (Grand Rapids: Eerdmans, 1947) .

Is it not high time that those of us who profess to believe that the whole Bible is the Word of God begin to demonstrate the practicability of that Word in the development of a sound social philosophy?[2]

Evangelist Billy Graham similarly wrote in his best-seller, *Peace with God*:

Jesus taught that we are to take regeneration in one hand and a cup of cold water in the other. Christians, above all others, should be concerned with social problems and social injustices.[3]

Over a decade later he wrote an answer to a question about the social gospel which elaborates this position:

I lay a great deal of emphasis on the social applications of the Gospel. For a Christian to ignore the social problems around him is a tragedy. . . . my first responsibility is to win men to Christ, then and only then can and will they live as Christians in the world. There have been Christians who have neglected their social responsibilities, but let us remember that almost all great social reforms have come through the application of Christian principles.[4]

Evangelical missionaries in underdeveloped nations increasingly recognize that Christians must actively combat disease, poverty, ignorance, and the economic, social, and political patterns which retard general progress and opportunity for the common people. Their spiritual responsibility includes social responsibility:

Neutrality on the part of the church would be construed as the negation of the redemptive truth we proclaim. . . . Social needs confront us and demand our decisions. We evangelicals are in the midst of them. We can no longer ignore social problems, nor can we evade our responsibilities.[5]

---

2 "Social Justice and Evangelical Christianity," *United Evangelical Action,* XIV (March 1, 1955), 10.

3 *Peace with God* (Garden City, N.Y.: Doubleday, 1953), p. 190.

4 "My Answer," *St. Paul Dispatch* (July 23, 1964), p. 20. (Reprinted by permission.)

5 Ruben Lores, "Why I Am Concerned about Social Needs," *The Christian Reader,* II (April-May, 1964), 23-25, reprinted from *Latin America Evangelist* (Nov.-Dec., 1961).

The Historical Background

Evangelical Christianity was a major influence on many social reforms in industrial societies during the eighteenth and nineteenth centuries. It had a profound impact upon the abolition movement, prison reform, the treatment of the mentally ill, and working conditions of industrial laborers in England ("factory reform").[6] The concern of evangelicals for human needs led to the establishment of many welfare societies which helped to alleviate the effects of social evils.[7]

Much zealous concern for social welfare can be traced to the compassion originally awakened by revivalists for sinning and suffering men. At least until the Civil War, the dominant note of evangelical preachers with regard to social issues was one of liberalism, not reaction. They recognized that sin is never solitary; personal sin often has its roots in society. The triumph of the gospel of Jesus Christ called for its victory over all evil, not merely for the deliverance of isolated persons from harm.[8]

Gradually, however, many religious leaders moved toward one or the other of two extremes. Some recognized that every social problem is closely linked with the motivations of individual persons, and hence they became very individualistic. They preached a gospel of personal piety, assuming that when the sins of individuals were corrected, the problems of society would be eliminated. Others saw the penetrating influence of social institutions, the high degree to which all persons are shaped by their environments, and the impact of general societal pressures upon the individual. These stressed the necessity of societal reform, for they realized that the evils incidental to the rise of an urban industrial society could not be overcome simply by individual repentance and salvation.

Both parties supported their views with biblical teachings and felt that their opponents were misguided. Their respective viewpoints on sin and social problems were linked with other views of biblical interpretation and theology, all of which reinforced the differences between "fundamentalists" and those who

6 Earle E. Cairns, *Saints and Society* (Chicago: Moody Press, 1960).

7 Charles I. Foster, *An Errand of Mercy* (Chapel Hill: University of North Carolina Press, 1960).

8 Timothy L. Smith, *Revivalism and Social Reform* (New York: Abingdon Press, 1957), esp. pp. 148-162.

believed in "the social gospel." Each group tended to see the other's teachings only as errors, fearing to endorse even their wholesome doctrines lest they suffer "guilt by association."

Social gospel leaders often failed to preach individual repentance and conversion, and fundamentalists often failed to recognize that a man can be so much a part of a social system that even when he is personally honest, responsible, dependable, kind, loving, and generous, the organization of which he is a part can be undermining Christian virtues and promoting cruel injustices to laborers, consumers, or other people. Both groups failed to recognize the practical significance and applications of many different but important teachings of the Bible. Their preconceptions blinded their eyes when they read Scripture passages contrary to their extremist positions, making them say in effect, "The Bible says this, but it really means that."

To be truly scriptural, we must see the need for both individual regeneration and Christian social concern. It is only as persons are born again by the Holy Spirit that they become spiritual children of God, but the gospel of Jesus Christ has far-reaching social implications. If Christians are "so heavenly-minded that they are of no earthly good," the gospel has been perverted. A realistic Christian framework will not be permeated by a theological dualism which assumes that the temporal and eternal worlds, or the body and soul, are so unrelated that God's sovereignty applies only to a future kingdom or only to man's spirit.

Both "religious individualism" and "social salvation" are in error, yet both perspectives contain elements of truth that must be emphasized and re-emphasized in order to uphold the gospel. Soul-winning and social concern go hand in hand in the Christian faith.

The Neglect of Social Concern

There are many reasons why evangelical Protestants have played down the social implications of the gospel. First, they have reacted against the errors of those theologically liberal religious leaders who identified the Christian message with a call to social reform. While it is true that the gospel is given to the world, it is addressed primarily to the individual person (see, e.g., John 3:16-21). There is no such thing scripturally as a "social gospel," for each man is personally accountable to God and salvation is personal. Nevertheless, this personal confrontation with God has certain social sources and effects which must not be overlooked.

Second, evangelicals have sometimes misinterpreted the prophecy that perilous times shall come in the last days so that "evil men and seducers shall wax worse and worse, deceiving, and being deceived" (II Tim. 3:13). They have pessimistically taken this to mean that no matter what Christians and other men do, conditions will go from bad to worse; therefore it is no use trying to do anything about social problems except to rescue souls through personal evangelism.

Third, there is the closely related fallacy of "either-or" reasoning. It is assumed that the "social" and "personal" aspects of the Christian message, as well as its "this-worldly" and "other-worldly" implications, are opposed as black is to white, and that conversion is solely "personal" and relevant primarily to the future life. This type of thinking is often a symptom of the "closed mind" and "authoritarian personality" which lie at the heart of many personal and social problems.[9] When Christians manifest these pathological symptoms they become social problems rather than a source of social healing.

A fourth cause is, again, closely related. Social implications of the gospel have been avoided because of the assumption that anything which is "social" is thereby not "spiritual." Since the church's message is a "spiritual" one, and the Kingdom of Christ is not of this world (John 18:36), that which pertains to "worldly" society is wrongly assumed to be outside the direct concern of the gospel.

Fifth, the "gospel of individual piety" has interfered with Christian social concern. Emphasis upon glorious truths of God's Word and work and upon the ultimate coronation of Jesus Christ as King of kings and Lord of lords has been used to escape from the pressures of existence in this life. All too often, waiting for His coming has taken the place of working until His coming.

Pietistic groups therefore embrace the world, as Rasmussen has indicated. Their faith gives them the illusion of escaping

---

9 See T. W. Adorno, *et al., The Authoritarian Personality* (New York: Harper, 1950), and Milton Rokeach, *The Open and Closed Mind* (New York: Basic Books, 1960).

from the world instead of putting them on guard against it, and hence they support all sorts of secular causes uncritically and unknowingly.

> The full Gospel has been strained through a sieve of self-serving anxiety, and the milk of Christian obligation to God and community has been thrown away while the cream of selfish reward is retained. . . . anxiety for one's own good and one's own salvation is the root source of sin. "He who seeks his life shall lose it."[10]

Individualism leads to an aloofness from social concern. This in turn results in an unchristian focus upon self, or at best a concern for only a narrow circle of fellow believers.

Sixth, evangelical churches have looked inward, seeing their own needs almost exclusively. They have stressed the fellowship of believers rather than the ministry of service.

Since many social welfare teachings of the New Testament emphasize "loving the brethren" and "doing good to the household of faith," it has been assumed that the social concern of Christians is limited to believers. Reacting against liberal doctrines which include the universal fatherhood of God and brotherhood of man, evangelicals have tended to forget that all men are brothers in the flesh even if not in the spirit. Thus they have failed to recognize that the Old Testament law and New Testament ethics emphasize love to neighbors — neighbors outside the Christian church as well as those within it.

Seventh, there is a deep-seated feeling among evangelicals that "politics is dirty." Since social action in democratic societies involves political activity, and political activity requires compromise and thus failure to achieve that which is ideal, it has been felt that the church's purity would be threatened by social action programs. But such persons fail to see that they thus sanction major evils by trying to shun minor flaws.

Eighth, other forms of "separation from the world" also help to account for social neglect. A modern form of monasticism has led some to try to live completely apart from worldly people and institutions, except for those which provide jobs and economic goods and services. To avoid contamination by

---

[10] Albert T. Rasmussen, *Christian Social Ethics* (Englewood Cliffs, N. J.: Prentice-Hall, 1956), p. 106.

sin, social life has been divorced from the spiritual life. Salvation has been presented as applying only to the "soul" of man. Withdrawal from all voluntary community institutions and even from political responsibilities as citizens has been a common result.

Christians who take this position forget numerous instructions of the Bible. They imply that their faith and testimony are so weak that the darkness of the world can overcome the light that is in them. They forget that contact with sinners is inevitable as long as men are in the world (I Cor. 5:10). Only by associating with nonchristians can Christians give them the gospel message.

A ninth and more disturbing reason for the neglect of social concern is a growing conformity to worldly standards. Evangelical Christians on the whole have been rising in the social class structure. As they have done so, they have become increasingly content with the basic social system in which they find themselves. They have gradually and quietly accommodated their religious doctrines to the materialistic patterns of personal and family life which Jesus strongly condemned as the "worship of mammon" (Matt. 6:24; Luke 16:13). By their refusal to participate in social reform movements, they have placed their blessing upon the selfishness and covetousness which lie at the core of much modern economic and political life.

Many evangelical spokesmen tend to condemn labor leaders and praise businessmen, to oppose social legislation in favor of "voluntary charity," and to support conservative political and economic perspectives. These biases reflect the inclination of a substantial proportion of evangelical Christians to identify themselves with the interests of wealth and power in society.

The "suburban captivity of the churches" has extended into evangelicalism. It helps promote blindness to the needs of underprivileged peoples, for once one has what he himself needs, he tends to be shielded from other people in need. He can also be strengthened in the false assumption that every victim of social problems is being punished for his own sins.

The instruction to "be not conformed to this world" (Rom. 12:2) has ramifications that go far beyond the personal behavior of individual Christians. Sanctioning the status quo by refusing to work for the reformation of society is the equivalent of saying that society is already "Christian" or that the gospel is powerless to change it. The close relationship of this attitude to an overarching "national religion" of the American Way of Life is obvious. Social, economic, and political reasons more than strictly religious ones make many Christians refuse to become involved in social action. They do not realize their strong attachment to worldly values.

All of these reasons for neglect of Christian social responsibility are closely related to sin, which is the tenth and basic factor. It is a sin not to be concerned about the needs of suffering mankind, and it is selfish to say that Christians must keep "pure" in God's sight by avoiding "worldly problems." Many church members do not even care much about the social needs of a Christian brother, so we cannot expect them to be concerned for persons outside the church fellowship.

Lack of Christlike compassion is a symptom of spiritual death. Wrapped up in selfish pursuits, sometimes using even church participation to advance socially, many church members assume that the essence of spirituality lies in church activities. Clinging to the husks of religious conformity, they have lost the kernel of true religion. Church participation itself sometimes serves to sanctify the "success story" of the person who has moved "from rags to riches," as if that were a major criterion of God's blessing.

The contemporary lack of concern for men's social needs is not primarily intellectual; it is spiritual in the most precise sense of that word. If a man has a genuine encounter with God, his life will be transformed from self-seeking and self-aggrandizement to social concern, a concern for other people. The truly born-again man who is filled with the Holy Spirit will have love as well as faith and hope; "the greatest of these is love" (I Cor. 13:13). Without love to man, faith in God is dead (I John 3:10-17; cf. Jas. 2:14-26).

When revival comes to God's people, social concern is a fruit of repentance. The errors of both extremist camps are corrected when God's will is given full sway.

Pitfalls of Christian Social Action

Christians are prone to give an unwarranted blessing to their own political and economic system. They assume all too readily that their own institutional patterns are the ideal for all peoples at all times. But just as past patterns of civilization have faded away, so it is possible that the pronounced changes which already have affected the American social and economic structure will eventually transform it altogether. This will not necessarily make our society either more or less Christian than it now is.

Christians must always beware of regarding institutional patterns as goals in themselves instead of means to the end of serving God. They should not assume, for example, that meeting the needs of one or more welfare programs within their denomination absolves them of other responsibilities toward society as a whole. Neither should they become so involved in programs of relief that they neglect to attack the social evils that continue to cause human distress.

Churches today are under pressures to "do something" because of evident social needs and the influence of groups which are organized to promote remedies for certain of those needs. They may be tempted to do a little in order to avoid the charge that they are irresponsible. At the same time they may face the opposite temptation not to act at all, for fear of the charge that the church has only a "spiritual" ministry and action is "worldly." In either instance, the church's action or inaction is likely to be opportunistic rather than principled, based on pressures of the moment rather than on carefully formulated policies.

More and more, Christians are called upon to join crusades to promote white supremacy, freedom riders, anti-Communism, civil liberties, laissez-faire economics, Christian socialism, constitutional government, pacifism, militarism, and a host of other causes. Public relations experts pushing these causes use Scripture references, names of respected Christian leaders, and other devices. They convey the impression that every sincere Christian ought to support their movement, agency, or organization.

Christians need always to remember, however, that not all who quote the Bible are truly scriptural (see Matt. 4:6). Not all who call themselves the followers, disciples, or servants of Jesus Christ are truly serving His cause (Matt. 7:21-23). Even a Christian theology does not guarantee correct insights into political, economic, or social phenomena, for now we know only in part (I Cor. 13:12), and the children of this age are often wiser than the children of light (Luke 16:8).

23

Theologically conservative Protestants have long been concerned with the social problems related to alcohol, tobacco, sex, Sabbath observance, cosmetics, divorce, gambling, political corruption, censorship of immoral books and magazines, and the like. Many of them now recognize the inconsistency of emphasizing these and at the same time disavowing any particular *Christian* interest in such other problems as poverty, unemployment, automation, nuclear warfare, mental illness, the population explosion, widowhood, racial conflicts, and crime. Recognizing past errors, facing the realities of the modern world, and accepting the social imperatives of the Christian gospel have led to a growing interest in developing an evangelical Christian social ethic.

Christians should be led individually and collectively by the Holy Spirit. If they claim to be followers of God, using the Bible illuminated by the Holy Spirit as their guide to faith and conduct, and then refuse to obey God's leading, they are involved in a form of hypocrisy, one of the sins most strongly condemned by Jesus Christ. Men must be doers as well as hearers of the Word of God.

In Christian social action, the Lordship of Jesus Christ must be the central focus of concern: we must "seek first the kingdom of God and his righteousness" (Matt. 6:33). If this unifying principle is observed, each part of the program will contribute meaningfully to the goals of the whole, while division and fragmentation will be avoided. Christian action should not be so unbalanced that minor needs are met conscientiously while major ones are totally neglected. The church should contribute to society by serving it, as Jesus did, instead of impoverishing it by draining time, resources, and personnel away from its valid functions.

Social concern must be seen in the context of the total society. It includes *social welfare*, aimed at alleviating problems of men, and *social action*, which includes welfare but is particularly aimed at reforming basic conditions through political or other processes. Giving financial or other aid to flood victims is an illustration of social welfare; working to pass a law to provide them with welfare aid or to promote conservation practices that will help prevent future floods is an illustration of social action.

The church's involvement in welfare and social action must

be seen in the context of its basic mission as the body of Christ in the world as well as in the light of its nature as an institution of society. It is only through an analytical process of abstraction that a church can be considered separate from its society. Similarly, a church's social concerns can be viewed as separate from all its other ministries only by a process of abstraction.

A Preview

In this book we shall try to see Christian social responsibility consistently from the perspectives of its place in the total life and work of the Christian church. We will stress general principles that apply to a wide variety of social problems and situations. It is not our purpose to survey specific social problems, but the generalizations given can be used in the evaluation of Christian perspectives bearing on any specific problem.

To help Christians discern God's will in regard to the social needs of mankind, the scriptural basis for social concern is presented in Part II, society's need in Part III, modes of implementing Christian social concern in Part IV, and some suggestions for the evaluation of church efforts in Part V. A persistent effort is made to present a viewpoint that is consistent with both the realities of the contemporary world revealed by the social sciences and the values of Christian faith revealed in the Bible.

No pretense is made that this book is "the last word" on the subject.[11] It is but a beginning. It will be the most profitable to the reader who studies its contents critically, compares them with other works on social ethics, and discusses them with other Christians in the light of specific environmental contexts. The suggestions for discussion and the references at the end of each chapter are intended to stimulate a meaningful, realistic, and practical investigation of Christian social responsibility.

11 Numerous topics touched upon could be greatly expanded. The social teachings of the Hebrew prophets, the history of welfare programs and social action projects in the Christian church, and the ministry of Jesus to people who were in social distress — all these could be explored at greater length. Practical programs of action, variations in social concern between denominations, and scientific knowledge that is related to social responsibility could also be extended into lengthy treatises. Almost all of the suggestions for discussion and study could be elaborated similarly. This book is only a brief presentation designed to stimulate thought and action; it should not be considered the last word on the subject.

SUGGESTIONS FOR DISCUSSION AND STUDY

1. Define social concern, social action, social ministries, social welfare, and social responsibility. Are any of these terms synonyms?

2. How do you reconcile the gospel of individual salvation with the social obligations of the gospel?

3. Use a concordance to look up all Bible passages in which the word "gospel" appears. What does it mean to believe, confirm, have fellowship in, impart, minister, obey, pervert, preach, and serve in the gospel? How is each of these related to Christian social responsibility?

4. Jesus implied in Matthew 7:13-14 that the majority of people are on the way to destruction. If he personally were to visit your community today, which common practices in economic, political, and social life would He commend, and which would He condemn? How can Christians avoid sinful conformity with the world in regard to disapproved practices?

5. Identify a religious group in your community which professes to take no position on the social problems and politics of your community. Which side of controversial issues does it support through its inaction? Is its lack of activity more helpful to the cause of good or of evil?

6. What position has your church taken on current political, economic, and social issues? Why? With what results? How does its position compare with that of other churches in your community?

7. Locate and compare several statements about Christian social responsibility. How are they similar? Can you explain or reconcile their differences?

8. Read one of Walter Rauschenbusch's books. Did he deny the importance of personal regeneration? Which of his ideas are clearly invalid today? Which are valid?

9. Study the history of the social gospel. Were its chief emphases based upon the Bible? Which of its assumptions and biblical interpretations are consistent with the doctrines of your church? Which are not? Why do churches seldom emphasize the social gospel today?

10. Read and evaluate Will Herberg's *Protestant — Catholic — Jew.* What evidence supports his conclusion that the American Way of Life is the operative faith of the American people and serves as a common denominator in a vague national religion? What evidence refutes it? Is evangelical Protestantism an exception? If so, could you prove it to Herberg's satisfaction?

RECOMMENDED READING

Bready, J. Wesley, *This Freedom — Whence?* New York: American Tract Society, rev. ed., 1942. A historical account of the evangelical Christian roots of social reforms, philanthropy, welfare, and human liberties.

Cairns, Earle E., *Saints and Society.* Chicago: Moody Press, 1960. The social impact of eighteenth-century English revivals and its contemporary relevance.

Carter, Paul A., *The Decline and Revival of the Social Gospel.* Ithaca, N. Y.: Cornell University Press, 1956. A history of social and political liberalism in American Protestant churches from 1920 to 1940.

Cross, Robert D., ed., *Walter Rauschenbusch: Christianity and the Social Crisis.* New York: Harper and Row, Torchbooks, 1964. A new edition of one of the "classics" of the social gospel movement; Rauschenbusch's book was originally published in 1907 by The Macmillan Co.

Herberg, Will, *Protestant — Catholic — Jew.* Garden City, N. Y.: Doubleday, Anchor Books, rev. ed., 1960. An interpretation of the religious situation in the United States.

Hopkins, Charles H., *The Rise of the Social Gospel in American Protestantism 1865-1915.* New Haven: Yale University Press, 1940. A history of the social gospel movement.

Smith, Timothy L., *Revivalism and Social Reform.* New York: Abingdon Press, 1957. An interesting historical study of the influence of revivalistic religion and the quest for Christian perfection on social reforms in mid-nineteenth-century America.

PART II:

THE SCRIPTURAL BASIS FOR CHRISTIAN
SOCIAL CONCERN

Chapter 2

The Gospel and Social Responsibility

And, behold, a certain lawyer stood up, and tempted him, saying, Master, what shall I do to inherit eternal life?

He said unto him, What is written in the law? how readest thou?

And he answering said, Thou shalt love the Lord thy God with all thy heart, and with all thy soul, and with all thy strength, and with all thy mind; and thy neighbour as thyself.

And he said unto him, Thou hast answered right: this do, and thou shalt live (Luke 10:25-28).

THE GOSPEL IS THE GOOD NEWS OF SALVATION IN AND THROUGH Jesus Christ. All of Christianity focuses on Christ, so the entire Christian message is included, directly or indirectly, in the gospel. This glorious gospel has numerous implications for Christian social concern, some of which will be surveyed here.

The gospel is eminently personal, for each man has his own encounter with God and chooses to accept or reject Him. But the gospel also is social, for every person is deeply enmeshed in a social situation, and it is impossible to love God while hating one's neighbor (I John 4:20-21). Neighborly love is always social; as soon as two persons are related in any way to each other, they are in a social relationship. There is therefore no such thing as a "personal gospel" apart from a "social gospel"; God's saving grace is extended to man in his social situation, not apart from it. Recognizing this is not the same as being caught up in a theologically liberal "social gospel." Only those who are born again will share in the eternal Kingdom of God (John 3:3-5).

The essence of the gospel is not ethics, yet we shall see that the gospel has profound ethical implications.

Basic Christian Doctrines and Social Responsibilities[1]

1. *God.* God is the Creator and the Sovereign of the universe. "In the beginning God created the heaven and the earth" (Gen. 1:1). "The earth is the Lord's, and the fulness thereof; the world, and they that dwell therein" (Ps. 24:1). Men are stewards, not owners, of their possessions. Their use of material things is under God's Lordship and judgment.

God's sovereignty is the chief foundation for Christian hope. This doctrine is implicitly denied by those who infer that the outcome of world history will be decided by the rulers of earth in either the free world or the nations behind iron and bamboo curtains.

God's sovereignty is a corrective to the despair of men who are dismayed by the wide scope and far-reaching effects of social problems. It also removes the pride of those who believe that their own economic or political system is the ultimate hope of mankind. The eternal triumph of the gospel of the grace of God through Jesus Christ should be reflected in all of the Christian's attitudes, words, and deeds, including his recommendations for the treatment of social problems.

God is righteous, generous, good, and just. His love is extended to the whole world, not merely to those who love Him. He calls upon His children to do justice, love mercy, and walk humbly with Him, actively loving even those who return only curses and hatred (Micah 6:8; Matt. 5:43-48). Like the father of the Prodigal Son, He runs to forgive His erring children and welcomes them back into the family circle (Luke 15:11-32). Christian social concern imitates God's concern. His love is a model to copy.

2. *Man.* "God created man in his own image" (Gen. 1:27). This fact is so profound that its implications have been the subject

---

[1] This section is only a brief summary of selected aspects of doctrine which have relevance to social concern. It is not intended to be a survey of Christian doctrine per se.

of extensive theological study and discussion throughout Judeo-Christian history. Man, like God, is a person. Man, like God, has intelligence and a will. Man, like God, is self-conscious. Unlike other living creatures, man is much concerned about who and what he is. All of his philosophies and religions are related to this quest for self-identification, which is basically a spiritual quest. "God is a Spirit" (John 4:24); man also is a spiritual being.

Man is monogenetic; that is, all people are descendants of Adam and Eve. All men are brothers in the flesh, and all are dependent upon others for their welfare. Social concern is irrevocably linked with the essential nature of man.

Why was man created? Biblical doctrines on this subject are summarized in church confessions which state that man was created "to glorify God and enjoy Him forever." Glorifying God includes, among other things, reflecting His love through social welfare projects bearing the burdens of others and through social action programs to prevent their future suffering.

God's concern for man is for the total person, not just a part. The Bible emphasizes that man is a unified total being, not merely an abstract, mystical, ghostly soul. The ancient Hebrew perspective saw the "soul" as the very essence of man. This "soul" is basically the same as what behavioral scientists today call the ego, self, or person. The person has both body and spirit — both seen and unseen aspects — but these can be separated from each other only for purposes of analysis. When they are divided, their separate parts do not adequately express or reflect the whole man. This fact is reflected in the words of Jesus when He healed the man who was paralyzed. He implied that "Man, thy sins are forgiven thee" and "Rise up and walk" are equally important statements (Luke 5:18-24). Bodily and spiritual needs exist together as inherent aspects of one human nature.

Modern speech patterns easily mislead us into the heretical position that only the "soul" of man, not the whole of man, is God's concern. This contributes to a pattern of "spiritualizing" biblical teachings, separating the soul from the remainder of man. God's love goes out to all of the person, as well as to all persons. The gospel is for the whole man. Its social implications cannot really be divided from the other components of spirituality.

Man is a social being. He is loved by God and judged by God as an individual, yet he is born into an earthly society which

33

greatly influences his attitudes, actions, and beliefs. Even his personal relationships with God are largely patterned by social experiences, for men cannot believe the gospel unless they hear it, "and how shall they hear without a preacher?" (Rom. 10:14). The Bible as we know it is the product of translators, printers, paper manufacturers, book binders, distributors, and a host of other people. No man lives to himself, and no man dies to himself (Rom. 14:7). Social concern grows out of the very nature of man.

Although man is largely a child of his environment, each individual also modifies his society, helping to change its beliefs and actions. The child of one generation is the father of the next. He who is influenced by his social circumstances is also an influence upon them.

Man, like God, is an autonomous being. He is dependent on others, but he also has a high degree of freedom from external control. He is free to choose for God or to rebel against Him, and free as well to make the lesser decisions of daily life.

Man's will is linked with his self-regulation. All of man's life, as well as all of the life of a group or society, is formed by choices. As men make choices, they become what they are. Choice-making continues throughout life, so there is a sense in which persons are always in the process of becoming. Indeed, the fact that processes are occurring is the very essence of life, whether it is seen from a biological, psychological, sociological, or spiritual perspective.

3. *Sin.* Man was created in God's image to live in fellowship with Him, but he destroyed this relationship by disobedience. The sins of pride, covetousness, and other forms of self-seeking also lie at the root of broken relationships between men. Human prejudice, poverty, and suffering grow out of man's sin.

God is not the source of sin. When He looked upon His finished creation, "God saw every thing that he had made, and, behold, it was very good" (Gen. 1:31). "Let no man say when he is tempted, I am tempted of God: for God cannot be tempted with evil, neither tempteth he any man: But every man is tempted, when he is drawn away of his own lust, and enticed. Then when lust hath conceived, it bringeth forth sin . . ." (Jas. 1:13-15).

The Scriptures say much about the "sins of the flesh," which we commonly identify with alcoholism and sexual immorality, but a careful study of the New Testament will reveal an even greater concern for "sins of the spirit" — pride, hatred, gossip, envy, exploitation of others, greed, materialism ("mammon worship"), evil thoughts, grasping for power, seeking advancement, and the like.   Jesus taught that inner thoughts and hidden desires are the foundation upon which action is built (Matt. 15: 18-20).   Adultery and murder can be committed in the heart (Matt. 5:27-28; I John 3:15).   The *failure* to love is the equivalent of hatred, and hatred is morally equivalent to murder (I John 2:7-11; 3:10-18).

"Sins of the spirit" have profound social dimensions. Many of them are ultimately social, even public, in their causes as well as their effects.   Refusal to love a neighbor of a different racial or national background may result from experiences in a society which passes traditional prejudices down from one generation to the next.

Evil may be perpetuated by persons who are highly moral in their personal relationships but whose very morality leads them to conform sinfully to social organizations of which they are a part.   The plea of Adolf Eichmann, when charged with guilt for the murder of Jews in World War II, was that he followed orders, as any good soldier would.   "Eichmannism" is much more widespread than most of us realize.   When a business corporation or labor union seeks gain for itself at the expense of the larger society, we praise its role in the free enterprise economic system. We sanction and participate in a greedy grasping for self-advantage in political campaigning that we as Christians would strongly condemn in an individual.   There are social sins as well as personal sins.   Man sins in his group action as well as in personal life.

This is not to imply that all current social problems can be assigned directly to sin. As we shall see in Chapter 4, the sufferers in our society are not necessarily worse sinners than other men. "All have sinned, and come short of the glory of God" (Rom. 3:23).   Furthermore, the vast number of social problems in the twentieth century does not necessarily prove that man is any worse today than he was in the past. Changes in social circumstances merely modify the patterns of sin. The underlying pattern of alienation from God and man remains, however, a basic cause of problems in all ages and societies.

Christian social concern aims at reconciling men to God and reconciling them to each other. Jesus Christ came "to seek and to save that which was lost" (Luke 19:10). He continues to say, "They that be whole need not a physician, but they that are sick. But go ye and learn what that meaneth, I will have mercy, and not sacrifice: for I am not come to call the righteous, but sinners to repentance" (Matt. 9:12-13).

4. *The Incarnation.* God has manifested Himself to men. He became flesh and dwelt among men, full of grace and truth (John 1:14). In response to man's need, God in Christ identified Himself with the human condition, including humiliation, temptation, poverty, and suffering (Luke 9:58; Phil. 2:6-8; Heb. 2:17-18; 5:8). His vicarious life and death, and above all His resurrection, is the good news of God's love in action. His own statement of the purpose of His ministry indicated that He was anointed to preach the gospel to the poor, heal the broken-hearted, proclaim deliverance to prisoners and restoration of sight to the blind, release the oppressed, and proclaim "the acceptable year of the Lord" (Luke 4:18-19). He identified Himself with the rich and the poor. He showed compassion for all men and met their physical as well as spiritual needs.

By becoming man, God confirmed the dignity and sacredness of humanity. Christian social concern is an outgrowth of His constraining love.

5. *Redemption.* Man's fellowship with God, broken by sin, can be restored through the saving life, death, and resurrection of Christ. Salvation includes the healing of broken relationships between a man and his neighbors. This restoration is in certain respects imperfect in this life because of the pervasive nature of sin, but it is nevertheless real. It is a present possession of the Christian believer who has committed himself to God through Jesus Christ, even as it is a future blessing to be bestowed upon him in all its fullness in the life to come.

The object of Christian social concern is wholeness, the "abundant life" of which Jesus spoke (John 10:10). It is only by the redemptive work of God's love that such salvation is accomplished. The redemptive concern that longs for complete reconciliation between man and God and between man and man is a motive of Christian welfare that cannot be overlooked.

As long as there is injustice, strife, crime, and other forms of man's inhumanity to man, reconciliation is incomplete. The person who has been born anew by God's Spirit, however, has a new outlook on life. The more he grows in grace, the more he will be concerned for his fellow men and the less he will center his attentions upon himself. He will work out his salvation, infusing temporal life with spiritual virtues by letting God work in him to do His good pleasure (Phil. 2:12-13).

6. *The Holy Spirit*. God the Holy Spirit is the agent of regeneration by which people become new creatures in Christ (John 3:5-8). It is He who teaches the Christian, reminding him at appropriate moments of the teachings of Jesus Christ (John 14:26) and guiding him into spiritual truth (John 16:13-15). He convicts the world of sin, righteousness, and judgment (John 16:8-11). He is the Spirit of Power dwelling in the Christian and enabling him to challenge the evils of his age (John 14:17; Acts 1:8; Rom. 8:9-11). The indwelling Spirit of God, who is Love, is the source of the love that gives the Christian a social passion (Rom. 5:5).

7. *Hope*. Hope is at the core of Christian faith, for "we are saved by hope" (Rom. 8:24). God makes men be born anew to a living hope and imperishable inheritance through the resurrection of Jesus Christ (I Pet. 1:3-4). Hope is a sure and steadfast "anchor of the soul" (Heb. 6:19), assuring us of our own resurrection and of the triumph of Christ's Kingdom over all dominions and powers, including death itself (I Cor. 15). All who await the "blessed hope" of Jesus' glorious return zealously purify themselves and live upright, godly lives (Tit. 2:11-14; I John 3:2-3).

Christian hope is oriented not only to the future; it is a present possession of those who trust in Jesus Christ. We know that human lives and social situations can be transformed by God's grace. The Christian hope declares that there is promise for even the most difficult situation which involves man in his estrangement from God. Hope is the sustaining force of social action and welfare. "Therefore, my beloved brethren, be ye stedfast, unmoveable, always abounding in the work of the Lord, forasmuch as ye know that your labour is not in vain in the Lord" (I Cor. 15:58).

8. *The Bible*. The Holy Scriptures are the basis for all Christian doctrine. The Bible is God's written Word revealing man's condition and his Redeemer, Jesus Christ. Illuminated by the Holy Spirit in the context of Christian fellowship, it is our sole guide to faith and conduct. What it says is therefore of utmost importance. Its pages from beginning to end are filled with direct and indirect instructions about Christian social responsibility.

All of these Christian doctrines are interrelated. They are reflected in every part of this book, but especially in the exhortations which follow in this chapter and the next.

The Biblical Call to Social Action

An echoing cry whenever men discuss social problems is the ancient question of Cain, "Am I my brother's keeper?" (Gen. 4:9). Sometimes, as in the case of Cain, it is asked with a note of defiance to justify or excuse sinful deeds. Sometimes it is asked in frustration as men look at the complex network of social institutions and the inescapable snare of human problems, wondering how they can ever do anything effective to alleviate suffering and promote good. Sometimes it is asked in humility by people with a genuine desire to do God's will in their relationships to their fellow men.

Answers to this question are found in the Bible all the way from Genesis to Revelation. The Old Testament Law and Prophets repeatedly refer to man's obligations to his fellow men. The teachings of Jesus Christ by word and example, experiences of the early Christians, and instructions in the New Testament Epistles all affirm that man is indeed his brother's keeper.

Imitating Jesus Christ. Christians are told to imitate Jesus Christ. His example involved serving others (Mark 10:45; Luke 22:27). He expressed the will of God by His actions even more than by His words. He fed the hungry, healed the sick, gave sight to the blind, restored strength to the crippled, and even provided refreshments for a wedding feast! His concern for the material and physical needs of man stands out prominently in the Gospels. Jesus was a friend of sinners (Matt. 11:19; Luke 7:34).

38

Jesus commanded those who believe in Him to follow Him; following is the essence of being His disciple (John 8:12, 31, 32; 10:27; 12:26; cf. Eph. 5:1-2 and I John 2:6). To be a Christian involves imitating the person of Christ, not simply obeying a law or code of ethics. What this implies is directly stated in many passages of Scripture (Mark 10:42-45; John 13:13-17; 15:12-14; Phil. 2:5-8; and I Pet. 2:21-24 are examples). Its practical implications are indirectly evident throughout the New Testament.

Obedience to God's Will. Jesus' Great Commission states that men should be taught to *observe* all that He has commanded (Matt. 28:19-20). The prayer the Lord taught His disciples includes the expression, "Thy will be done in earth" (Matt. 6:10). The Christian is created a new creature in Christ for the very purpose of engaging in good works (Eph. 2:8-10). He is sanctified unto obedience (I Pet. 1:2) and instructed to let his light so shine that men will see his good works and glorify God as a result (Matt. 5:16). He is taught that faith without works is dead, being alone (Jas. 2:14-18). A balanced emphasis upon both faith in Jesus Christ and works for Jesus Christ is necessary to fulfill God's will. In order to obey the expressed will of God, one must have an active concern for social problems.

Judgment of the Nations. The only judgment which Jesus directly described emphasizes a separation of the "sheep" from the "goats" on the basis of social action. The nations will be asked whether they fed the hungry, gave drink to the thirsty, welcomed the stranger, clothed the naked, visited the sick, and visited the prisoners. Inasmuch as these things are done to the very *least* of Jesus' brethren, they are done unto the King (Matt. 25:31-46; cf. Mark 9:33-50). The "brethren" referred to here include all members of the human race, not solely those who are brothers in the added sense of being born again. Jesus identified Himself with the whole of humanity by carrying the burden of sin of all mankind.

The Greatest Commandment. God's will in the area of social concern can be summarized under the one instruction to *love*. Loving God and loving men summarizes all of God's will for all men. To serve God, one *must* serve his fellow men (I John 2:10—3:18). "God is love" (I John 4:8). He calls all Christians to love, to partake of His very nature, which is love.

Possibly the clearest description of what love to one's neighbor really means is in the account of the Good Samaritan (Luke 10:23-37). In answer to the question, "Who is my neighbor?" Jesus explained that the real question is, "To whom will you be neighbor? To whom will you show mercy?" I am neighbor to anybody whom I help, even if he is of a different social class or nationality and lives in a distant place. The priest and the Levite who passed by the victim of thieves did not show love, but the Samaritan who had compassion proved himself to be neighbor.

Love is the fulfillment of the Law; the royal law which summarizes all others is that one shall love his neighbor as himself (Matt. 5:43-48; 22:36-40; Gal. 5:14; Jas. 2:8; etc.). The one who loves owes no one anything, for he fulfills all of the Law (Rom. 13:8-10). Moreover, love among Christian brethren has clear evangelistic implications, for it demonstrates to all men that certain people are the disciples of Jesus Christ (John 13:34-35). Christians are to make love their aim (I Cor. 14:1).

The Works of Love. Love affects relationships with other people, for it is not just an inward set of attitudes. Love as described in I Corinthians 13 is very practical and active; it is not merely "in the heart." Love that ends there is not love at all. *Agape* love is "love in action," the only truly Christian kind of love. It stands in clear contrast to the popular "sentimental slush" of romanticized love, which is a perversion of true Christian love. Love involves activity, not just attitudes; deeds, not just devotion; works, not just worship; fact, not just faith. A "love for souls" that neglects the body is a greedy perversion seeking selfish rewards.

Faith works by love (Gal. 5:6). It is by love that Christians serve one another (Gal. 5:13). Men should not be weary in well-doing, but should, to the extent of their opportunities, do good to all men (Gal. 6:9-10). The fruit of the Spirit focuses strongly upon relationships to other people, although it grows out of an inward relationship to Christ which enables the Christian to be led by the Holy Spirit (Gal. 5:16-26).

This emphasis upon loving one's neighbor is characteristic of Hebrew as well as Christian ethics. New Testament instructions to love grow out of an Old Testament background (Exod. 20:12-17; Lev. 19:17-18; Deut. 15:7-11). The enemy was to be loved, not only friends (Exod. 23:4-9; Lev. 19:33-34). Hebrews were to treat strangers in their midst as they treated themselves; all human beings were to be respected. The Old Testament prophets emphasized mercy and justice, both of which prevent the institutionalization of hatred and denial of love.

God's Example. God demonstrates his love to man by letting His blessings fall upon the unrighteous as well as upon the righteous. God loves the unworthy. The Christian should, like God, love his lazy, seemingly irresponsible, maladjusted, ungrateful, profligate neighbor. God calls His children to love not only "the worthy" and the good who will return thanks but also the unworthy who may never demonstrate or express gratitude (Matt. 5:43-48; Luke 6:27-36).

Inasmuch as God so greatly loves the world, His children should love it too.

Motives for Social Concern

Other biblical teachings also imply that Christians should have a social concern. If one is filled with the Holy Spirit, he will share Christ's compassion for his fellow men. The love of Christ will constrain him to act. Out of gratitude for God's unmerited favor, he will pour unmerited favors upon his fellow men.

Moreover, the church's concern for evangelism offers reasons for an active social witness. When a Christian performs good deeds and gives God the credit, men will be led to glorify Him for the contrast between the typical man of the world and the Christian who loves his neighbor as himself (Matt. 5:16). As God's love to men is demonstrated by acts of kindness, the good deeds of men are sermons even if no advertising "commercial" is pinned to the acts of mercy and love.

Evangelism is indirectly woven into Christian social action in many other ways. If a man is hungry, suffering from pain, or anxious about the material well-being of his family, the pressures of his economic, physical, or social burden will prevent him from hearing the gospel when it is proclaimed to him. Meeting other needs in the name of Christ removes this barrier. It proves the sincerity of the evangelist's love.

Even though Christian social action is not oriented toward evangelism as its primary goal, yet it is part of the total task assigned by Christ. In performing that task, Christians will plant and water seeds that will yield a spiritual increase given by God (see I Cor. 3:5-11). Social reform and social welfare are aspects of proclaiming the gospel.

Subchristian motivations may get involved in Christian social concern. Sometimes the building of a strong church, board, or agency becomes a major goal for action. When this becomes an end in itself, instead of a means to the end of serving God and men, it is a form of idolatry. If one accepts social responsibility simply because he wants to receive personal rewards in this life or in the life to come, he is self-seeking and self-centered.

Selfishness may take several forms. One may support a retirement home because he wants it to be available in case of later personal need. He may engage in "works of righteousness" to demonstrate his generosity and receive the praise of men. He may be active in social programs because of the wholesome influence they will have upon some institution whose growth will reflect favorably upon him. He may promote social welfare in order to win converts to Christ so that stars will be added to his heavenly crown. He may help another person in order to receive expressions of gratitude which inflate his own ego. When "love" is expressed primarily for the sake of direct personal returns, it may not be love at all!

Yet to love one's neighbor as oneself, one must love oneself. As long as one seeks for his neighbor the same benefits as he seeks for himself, he is not necessarily acting in an unchristian manner. But when his "loving concern" becomes merely the lure of a trap into which other people are manipulated for the advantage of the "concerned" person, the ulterior motive tends to shine through the deeds and the person "helped" is likely to become resentful. True Christian love is given to men as they are, not because of what they have achieved or may contribute to others.

Self-righteous persons or those unconsciously carrying a load of guilt often alienate people in need because their motives for service are confused. Without realizing it, they try to solve their personal problems through helping others; they are manipulating people for self-advantage. Such persons may do more harm than good if they enter the helping professions or engage in volunteer services.

We may be tempted to say that Christians should not get involved in social ministries unless their motives are pure. But motives are always an admixture of many elements, some of which are self-centered. An act of kindness is a kind act even if done out of imperfect motives. It is far better to do good out of imperfect motives than not to do good at all!

The Christian is in a better position than other men to help meet social needs, for God can give him compassion for the unlovely, an inner constraining love that results in outer acts of love. Even when good is done out of imperfect motives, let us be like the Apostle Paul. When some preached Christ because of envy and strife, he rejoiced as long as Christ was preached (Phil. 1:12-18).

Love Demands Action

God's love extends to all areas of human need. It is not limited to the "spiritual" life of man in the narrow sense of that term, nor to only a few areas of social welfare. To love as we have opportunity unquestionably involves all sorts of personal relationships, meeting the needs of persons near us who are caught in troubles of any kind. Personal comfort is most effectively offered when we ourselves have been comforted by God in any affliction (II Cor. 1:3-7). But Christian love goes beyond this to meet the personal needs of people whom we do not see, even those on the opposite side of the earth.

Love necessitates concern for social needs — needs that are shared by numerous people in a society. It has been relatively easy for Christians to express concern for the plight of individual persons when they suffer, but somehow it has been difficult for many to see that that plight is often a product of social circumstances. Unless those basic conditions are corrected, persons will continue to be their victims. Hence Christian love also directs its attention to the basic conditions which cause social problems. Social action in a democratic society takes places largely through political institutions. Such activity may seem highly "depersonalized," but it profoundly affects personal experience (see Chap. 4). The gospel is social because it is personal. Biblical individualism includes social concern.

To love one's neighbor as oneself implies a high standard of personal ethics. The one who truly loves will not cheat on his income tax returns, for if he does, someone else will have to bear a higher proportion of the tax load. He will not waste material resources and thus deprive a present or future neighbor. He will not be selfish in his political behavior, for love will make him desire for his neighbor the same advantages he would like to have himself. He will, in other words, love in deed and not in word only. His love will be evident in daily conduct at every level of life — occupational, recreational, economic, religious, social, familial, and even personal.

Love does not always mean the kind of action that it might at first glance seem to imply. Scientific research and the experience of people in the "helping professions" can clarify love's demands. Psychology can provide knowledge about human motivations and responses. Sociology can describe the effects of various kinds of social action. Psychiatry can furnish techniques and skills of identifying and treating emotional disorders. Social work reveals principles of helping others effectively. Other behavioral sciences and professions can promote Christian love in a wide variety of ways, preventing us from doing harm when we attempt to do good.

SUGGESTIONS FOR DISCUSSION AND STUDY

1. In what way is love the fulfillment of the law (Rom. 13:10)? Can you think of anything God has revealed as His will that cannot be included under love?

2. Study the "works of the flesh" and the "fruit of the Spirit" in Galatians 5:16-26. How does each of these vices and virtues relate to love? How many of them involve relationships with one's fellow men?

3. Read several translations of I Corinthians 13. Which of its statements about love apply to relationships with other people? Which emphasize activity, in contrast to attitudes?

4. Have you ever known of an incident in which love failed to have a healing effect for people with problems? Did the motives of the giver influence this failure? How? What was the recipient's interpretation of the situation?

5. To what extent is selfishness a motive for the welfare activities sponsored or approved by your church? Is such selfishness sinful? Can man ever do a completely selfless deed?

6. Does the judgment of the nations or peoples described in Matthew 25:31-46 have anything to do with collective deeds of "we the people" in a society which has democratic political institutions?

7. Who shares the guilt for depriving loyal American citizens with Japanese ancestry of their property and liberty when they were herded into concentration camps ("Relocation Centers") in 1942? Who is guilty for the thousands of human casualties inflicted by modern warfare? Who is responsible to God for the hundreds of thousands killed and maimed by the atomic bombs exploded on Hiroshima and Nagasaki in 1945? How are these questions related to "social sin"?

8. Should Christians praise the underground railway of pre-Civil War days which enabled slaves to escape, thus depriving their masters of wealth invested in human property? When there is doubt, should property rights have priority over human rights? Why or why not?

9. During the military occupation of World War II, many Danish, Dutch, Norwegian, and other patriots in occupied countries joined the "resistance movement" in opposition to their Nazi rulers. Since a Christian should be subject to his government (Rom. 13:1-7), is it right for him to resist the ruling authorities in this manner? What should a Christian soldier in Germany have done when commanded by his superior officers to march civilian Jewish prisoners to their death in a crematorium?

10. Make a list of the laws given God's people in the Old Testament pertinent to their treatment of strangers, visitors, gentiles, and other outsiders who had peaceful relationships with them. How did the prophets clarify these laws? What do these commandments imply about the Christian's love to his neighbor? How do they compare with instructions in the New Testament?

RECOMMENDED READING

Bachmann, E. Theodore, editor, *The Activating Concern: Historical and Theological Bases*. New York: National Council of the Churches of Christ in the U.S.A , 1955. Vol. I of *Churches and Social Welfare*. A background document for the National Conference on the Churches and Social Welfare which summarizes the social activities of thirteen Protestant denominations and their theological foundation.

Lunger, Harold L., *The Bible and Our Social Responsibility*. St. Louis, Mo.: The Bethany Press, 1958. A study course on the scriptural basis for and character of Christian social responsibility.

Schrey, Heinz-Horst, *et al.*, *The Biblical Doctrine of Justice and Law*. London: SCM Press, Ltd., 1955. A study on the theology of law.

Troeltsch, Ernst, *The Social Teaching of the Christian Churches*, trans. from German by Olive Wyon. New York: The Macmillan Co., 2 Vols., 1931. A historical survey and sociological interpretation of Christian doctrines and practices on social issues beginning with Jesus and the Apostolic Church.

Wright, G. Ernest, *The Biblical Doctrine of Man in Society*. London: SCM Press, Ltd., 1954. A biblical study of the individual's relationships and responsibilities in the community and world.

Chapter 3

Christian Stewardship and Social Concern

For unto whomsoever much is given, of him shall be much required: and to whom men have committed much, of him they will ask the more (Luke 12:48b).

No man can serve two masters: for either he will hate the one, and love the other; or else he will hold to the one, and despise the other. Ye cannot serve God and mammon (Matt. 6:24).

Moreover it is required in stewards, that a man be found faithful (I Cor. 4:2).

The Biblical Doctrine of Stewardship

THE BASIS FOR CHRISTIAN STEWARDSHIP LIES IN THE FACT THAT God owns everything (Exod. 19:5b; I Chron. 29:14; Ps. 24:1; 50:10-12; 89:11-12). Not only one-tenth of what we receive is His; the tenth is given as an indication of the fact that all belongs to Him. He owns all human beings as well as all things (Deut. 32:6; Ezek. 18:4; Acts 17:26). By creation all men are brothers. Christians, however, are owned by God in a special way — they are His by redemption as well as by creation (Rom. 14:8-12; I Cor. 6:19-20; etc.). Acknowledgment of Him as the Lord of all is a recognition of His ownership of oneself and of all things.

God has entrusted His creation to men (Gen. 1:28; 9:2; Ps. 8:6-8; Heb. 2:8). Individuals have varying numbers of opportunities as well as of things (Matt. 25:14-30; Luke 12:48; Rom. 12:3; I Cor. 12:7; etc.). Each will be held accountable personally for his stewardship of all that has been entrusted to him (Matt. 12:36; 18:23; Luke 12:48; 19:11-27; Rom. 14:12; II Cor. 5:10; Ezek. 18:20; etc.). To whom much is given, of him shall much be required. This accountability extends into every area of life, including political responsibilities, daily work, community life, family affairs, recreational behavior, and the like. It is not limited to activities directly associated with the organized church.

Conscientious application of the doctrine of stewardship breaks down the division between "holy" or "sacred" and "profane" or "secular" occupations and activities. Every legitimate vocation and every proper activity of the Christian is sacred. This means that being a Christian involves a special kind of life — a life completely dedicated to the service of the Lord, a life of praying without ceasing, a life which is "in Christ" and hence is an outworking of Christ's will day by day. The Christian will therefore approach social problems in a significantly different way than the person who is not a believer. As a member of the church of Jesus Christ, he will strive to be not conformed to the world (Rom. 12:1-2). He will play a leading role in pointing out features of society which seem contrary to God's will. He will identify stumbling blocks to faith in Christ, sources of human suffering, abuses of natural resources, and violations of the dignity of men created in the image of God. Just as Jesus went about doing good, the Christian will go about doing good.

Christian stewardship also imposes responsibilities upon men as members of groups, and hence upon the decisions and deeds of the groups themselves. The members who comprise a group are responsible for its acts and will give account of themselves before God. God's chief requirement is faithfulness (Matt. 25:21, 23; I Cor. 4:2). In relationship to social problems, faithfulness demands involvement in social welfare, participation in social action, and implementation of social concern.

Each church congregation and denomination, then, has a God-given task. Each has unique opportunities, for no two churches have identical social environments and historical backgrounds upon which to build their work. Churches, like individuals, are under the refining and corrective judgment of God; they have stewardship responsibilities (see Rev. 2:1-3:22). We will survey some of these, but first let us clarify certain relevant aspects of the nature of the church and the work that God has entrusted to it.

The Nature of the Church

The church is ideally a community or fellowship of believers gathered together from the world by God. They are members of the universal Church of Jesus Christ as well as of their local congregations. They are in the world, but their citizenship is in heaven (Phil. 3:20), so "they are not of the world" (John 17:16). Each member of this "gathered church" has personally responded to the call of Jesus Christ.

This concept of the church as an *ecclesia* can be misconstrued, however. It makes it easy to forget that man is a social as well as a psychological being. The church of Christ is a "household of faith." It is an organism in which all the members are inter-related and interdependent (I Cor. 12). It is a community which receives its life-giving and life-sustaining power from Jesus Christ. In relationship to the church, Christ is the root from which the vine receives its nourishment (John 15:1-6), the head from which the body receives direction (Eph. 5:23), the shepherd by whom the sheep are led (John 10:11-18; Heb. 13:20), the sun which is their source of light (John 1:4-5; 8:12; Eph. 5:8-14), the foundation upon which the entire building rests (I Cor. 3:11; Eph. 2:19-22). Each of these analogies is incomplete by itself and can be misleading if it is taken too rigidly as a picture of the relationship between Jesus Christ and His people. Yet each conveys a significant lesson — a lesson which among other things censures extreme individualism and emphasizes the inter-relationships between Christian people.

Overemphasis on the "gathered church" can make Christians callous to the needs of society at large. As a fellowship of believers, the church program may be organized around members' social and psychological needs to the exclusion of their responsibilities as members of the social organism called society.

This distortion of the concept of the gathered church violates God's commandment to love our neighbors as we love ourselves. Not only does the church *have* a ministry to the surrounding world, but the church is in the world to serve mankind, just as Jesus Christ was. The church *is* ministry. It exists to meet the needs of people not yet gathered into its fellowship as well as the needs of those who are. Each church has a parish, a community or area of the world to which it has special responsibilities.

When a church is made a fortress protecting itself from evil, it can easily forget that it has a ministry as an army to go forth and conquer evil in the name of Jesus Christ. When it becomes a pietistic sect which retreats from the world to keep itself "unspotted," it tends to become irrelevant and stained by sins of omission. When it is made a sheltering institution protecting insecure people from strangers in "the lonely crowd" of the surrounding society, a church easily becomes a ghetto which fails to accomplish its ministry for Jesus Christ. When a church is insulated and isolated from the world through a ministry which is exclusively to "souls," it has distorted the Christian message. When it looks through stained glass windows which prevent it from seeing people in need in its own Jerusalem and Judea, the multitudes for whom Christ had compassion and wept, it has abdicated its position as the hands, feet, and voice of Jesus Christ in the world to do His work, run His errands, and speak His Word to suffering and lost mankind.

The church is the "body of Christ" in the world (Rom. 12:4-8; I Cor. 12:12, 27). It has the significant task of making the gospel of Jesus Christ, who is the Word of Life and God Himself, become alive, relevant, and "incarnate" in the complex world of the twentieth century. The social dimension of man's relationships to men is an integral part of the gospel. Without it the gospel will not be the gospel, a life-giving and life-enriching force in the contemporary world. For this reason the Christian church must have an active social concern. It declares God's wonderful love by its deeds as well as by its words.

The Work of the Church

The church's task is to worship, witness, and work. Its goal is to bring wholeness, health, and holiness to men. Many Scripture passages clarify its work. Our attention will be focused upon those aspects which are particularly relevant to social concern.

Evangelism. The church has been given the significant task of evangelizing the world. Social service is one form of evangelism. Welfare activities demonstrate love. They help to prepare people to listen to the gospel by removing the barriers of problems that hinder them from hearing its proclamation. Christians must *be* the love of Christ in order to be heard when they speak about it. The church teaches by doing; its involvement in social welfare tells people of the world that it shares God's love for all men. The godly, holy living of its members is the equivalent of a witness to the Light of Life. Social action is thus an instrument of evangelism. It is also a result of evangelism which imparts to men the compassion of Christ.

The evangelistic aspects of social ministries are easily abused as a result of the sinful tendencies which are present even in the lives of redeemed men (I John 1:8; Rom. 7:13-25). Christians are tempted to use social services as a kind of bait in their work as "fishers of men." We tend to forget that our Lord did good to all men, with no conditional strings attached. He did not use people deceitfully by serving them with ulterior motives. When only one of the nine lepers He had healed returned to give Him thanks, He gave the man a special blessing but did not take back His help from the other nine (Luke 17:11-19). If we truly share the mercy of God and the love of Christ, our deeds of kindness will not be instruments of trickery like modern advertising "gifts." As we ourselves have freely received innumerable gifts from God and men, we will freely give.

Education. The church must teach children and adults in its educational program to observe all things Christ has commanded (Matt. 28:20). It teaches the world by its example of employment policies, services to retired and disabled employees, and relationships to national and community affairs. Its teaching ministry in bringing up its children, edifying its members, and influencing outsiders cuts across all of its other services. What it *does* in the area of human need teaches as much or more than what it *says*.

Service. Like its Lord, the Christian church is among men as one who serves (Luke 22:24-27). Just as Jesus laid down His life in service, His church has the task of ministering in love. When it forgets this responsibility and is made into an organization to be served by men, it becomes a "god" which supplants the place of the one true God. The church that is so busy administering routine programs of self-service that it can find no time and energy to serve unpredictable and unscheduled needs which suddenly arise in its own neighborhood is missing its high

51

calling in Christ. Jesus grasped the hand of the needy who interrupted His activities. His church should likewise lift the fallen.

The first "elders" or "deacons" were chosen in order to meet welfare needs (Acts 6:1-7). As a result of this formal organization, the Word of God increased and the church grew. Numerous passages in the Acts of the Apostles and in the Epistles reflect the welfare ministries of the early church. If we were to copy directly the program of the apostolic church, every congregation would have elders, deacons, or a social action committee actively and continuously engaged in tasks related to man's social needs.

Prophecy. The church has a prophetic function of speaking to men as the mouthpiece or spokesman of God. In preaching God's Word, the church gives society ethical guidance as well as the message of redemption. Standards of morality are formed and applied on the basis of the Ten Commandments and other biblical teachings. These standards guide economic, educational, political, scientific, welfare, family, and other institutions.

The church today should reclaim its enlightening role as the "conscience of society," indicating to the world what is right and wrong. The growing recognition that science in and of itself cannot provide these values is giving the ethical religions an open door of opportunity.

As the voice of God in the world convincing men of righteousness, sin, and judgment, the Christian church needs the correctives of sound theology, historical understanding, and a realistic knowledge of contemporary society. Otherwise self-appointed false prophets posing in the name of "true religion" will mislead Christians and others who are seeking light for life's pathway.

If the church were properly fulfilling its prophetic task, it would be impossible for its members to stand silently by when moral principles of the Decalogue are openly and officially violated in political, economic, and other institutions of society.

The prophetic role of the church includes confronting society with its imperfections, sin, and guilt, and reminding men of sin's consequences. To assume that one's own social order is perfect and that all other societies should be conformed to its image is a form of idolatry which makes ultimate that which is imperfect and temporary. No man has a lasting kingdom on earth; the Christian's eternal citizenship is in God's Kingdom.

Another aspect of the church's prophetic task is the identification of human needs. Historically the church has been a pioneer in the area of social welfare. Despite the abuses of almsgiving in medieval and modern history, the church was actively behind much valuable assistance in meeting the material needs of the poor, the crippled, the blind, and others who suffered.

The compassion of Jesus Christ ought to make Christians the pioneers in social action even in the contemporary world. A welding together of Christian moral sensitivity, full knowledge of men's problems and needs, and understanding of the channels through which society operates to meet needs should enable Christians to be in the forefront of social reform and welfare movements.

Sometimes the conflicting demands of pressure groups will introduce doubt about the specific stand that a church ought to take. When the social situation is such that sides *must* be taken on political and other issues, however, the church in justice ought to stand up for the weak, the poor, and the exploited, just as Jesus Christ and the prophets did, for such people are underrepresented and often totally unrepresented in legislative chambers and the halls of justice. The church should not become identified with any one social class; it should not be partial. It should never become a spokesman for the powerful vested interests of society, but neither should it become the voice for revolutionary groups which try to use the church to promote their selfish ends. Every church must take care to discharge its stewardship responsibilities faithfully in accord with the written Word and the Holy Spirit's enlightenment.

The Church as People

Where is your church on Monday through Saturday? Always on the same corner if the church is only a building. But that is not the essence of the church; a church is not primarily a building. Neither is it an abstract gathering which is "the church" only on those occasions when there are meetings in a church building. The church consists essentially of the people of God. These people are in the world, coming apart from it for fellow-

53

ship and worship only a few hours of the week. At those hours it is the "gathered church." All the other hours of the week its members are separated from each other. Nevertheless, they still comprise the church.

The work of the church is done primarily through its members. As the people of God in the world, the "scattered church" has the significant task of promoting the work of Jesus Christ, which is the work of the church, through everything they do. They are His representatives, ambassadors to extend His Lordship in a ministry of reconciliation (II Cor. 5:17-21). They are the "light of the world" reflecting the Sun of Righteousness; their light will be ineffective unless it is revealed to the world (Matt. 5:14-16). They are the "salt of the earth" with a preserving and purifying influence without which society would deteriorate (Matt. 5:13). Salt is ineffective when kept in a box on the shelf. So, too, the church's influence on society will be ineffective if it is not scattered into all the world. Wherever its members are at work, the church is at work.

The "church pillar" is not necessarily the best member of the body of Christ. If his concern is only with the church organization and not with the primary purposes for which that organization exists, he has lost sight of the church's mission. Unfortunately, goal displacement of this kind is fairly common. Christians too often think that their only work for Jesus Christ is what is done within the organizational structure of the church. The wrong kind of emphasis upon "church work" easily leads to the unchristian assumption that the other areas of life are "secular" and unrelated to Christian commitment.

Every Christian has a ministry. Each has received different gifts with which to minister to the common good (Rom. 12:3-8; I Cor. 12; I Pet. 4:10-11). One of the chief tasks of pastors and teachers is to equip and perfect other Christians for the work of their ministry (Eph. 4:11-16).

Christian laymen also can help one another to grow in the grace and knowledge of Jesus Christ so that they will become more effective servants of God (Heb. 10:24-25). Much of this is done within conventional church activities, but it can be done even more effectively through small groups. One pastor who has worked with Bible study groups testified:

No matter how academically I would start the discussion, the people would invariably bring it down to their daily lives where they needed help. We began to see that this experience was providing real Christian fellowship, more fellowship in Christ than any other group or work going on in our church.[1]

Many churches would benefit by reduced emphasis upon large-scale meetings in the church building and more stress upon small groups of persons who can give each other mutual support and help for their daily tasks as ministers of Jesus Christ. Such activity might even lead to a renewed emphasis upon "the church in thy house" (Philem. 2). It would help Christians to recognize that the church is primarily people and that every layman has a Christian ministry.

The Priesthood of the Believer

The doctrine of the priesthood of all believers (I Pet. 2:5, 9; Rev. 1:6; 5:10; 20:6; etc.) needs to be rediscovered and redeveloped. It has significant implications for the social ministry of the Christian church.

The priesthood of believers is not the purely individualistic concept that it is sometimes interpreted to be. Even the word *priest* implies a religious system with a social framework of relationships between people, not merely between a person and God. It is in this institutional context that a priest conducts religious rituals on behalf of others as well as himself.

The Christian is a "priest." As such, he is a member of a community of believers, all of whom are accountable to God, mutually responsible to one another, and servants of the society around them. He offers sacrifices of praise, thanksgiving, and good deeds to God (Heb. 13:15-16). He presents himself as a living sacrifice to serve God and man (Rom. 12). He intercedes with God on behalf of fellow men, both Christians and nonchristians (I Tim. 2:1-3). He has a ministry of reconciliation (II Cor. 5:17-21).

Serving God, serving one another, and serving other men strengthens the fellowship of the believers. In their fellow-

1 Robert A. Raines, *New Life in the Church* (New York: Harper and Row, 1961), p. 84.

55

ship each helps to inspire and instruct the others. As a result, they can proclaim the gospel more effectively through deeds and words wherever they go.

Conclusion

Christians are individually and collectively accountable to God for their life and service. It is their duty to be obedient to Him. What God has revealed to be His will is the binding commitment of the church. His love is the constraining force that leads them into service. His power is the enabling force that makes good works possible.

We recognize, of course, that the actual church, the church as it is observed and experienced by men, is not the ideal church. The ideal, however, should always be the goal toward which the church as an institution on earth steadily moves. As it does so, deeds of mercy, personal morality, and high standards of social ethics will characterize its evangelistic, educational, and service tasks.

To serve its present age in the spirit of Jesus Christ, the church's mission must be socially as well as personally regenerative. Otherwise the salt has lost its savor and is good for nothing except to be cast out and trodden under the feet of men, who will scorn it and reject its Lord. If this is the only product of its efforts, the heavy hand of God's judgment will rest upon it, for it will have failed in its stewardship responsibilities.

SUGGESTIONS FOR DISCUSSION AND STUDY

1. Why does the word "stewardship" usually imply a discussion of tithes and offerings for Christian causes? What is valid about that perspective? What invalid impressions accompany the monetary interpretation of stewardship?

2. What is meant by the statement that the church is a social institution? Is the Christian church *only* a social institution?

3. What do money-raising dinners, bazaars, and carnivals teach the world about the nature and ministry of the church? What kinds of motives are appealed to by the guessing games, attendance contests, trading stamps, and novelty acts which are some-

times used to promote church programs? What is their educational impact? Summarize the arguments for and against their use.

4. How is the acceptance of Jesus Christ as Saviour related to accepting His Lordship over every aspect of personal and social life? Is faithful Christian stewardship essential to salvation?

5. How may a person's economic, physical, psychological, and social problems be barriers to hearing the gospel? Is the mentally ill, diseased, intoxicated, distressed, hungry, unemployed, or indigent person more likely to respond to an evangelistic invitation to make a decision for Christ before or after his physical and material needs have been met? Why? Can you cite illustrations of specific cases?

6. Use a concordance to locate the New Testament passages that refer to prophecy, prophesying, prophets, and related concepts. What is the nature of prophecy in the Christian church? What does this imply for the prophetic ministry of your church?

7. Read Amos, Micah, Habakkuk, Malachi, or one of the major prophets (Isaiah, Jeremiah, Ezekiel). Identify the specific social evils they condemned. Are any of these conditions present in the modern world? If so, is God's message about them modified in any way, or is it still the same as in the days of the Hebrew prophets?

8. Do a church's stewardship responsibilities demand that it attempt to minister to *all* people in its community? Are there any biblical grounds for a refusal to minister to people from certain social classes, racial groups, nationalities, occupations, educational backgrounds, or religious heritages who are in the vicinity of a church?

9. Can a church compromise its prophetic message to society by its actions? Do its business affairs ever give the world a message that is contrary to the spoken words of the church? (Consider matters like fees for the use of its building, salaries of the minister and other employees, honoraria to guest speakers and musicians, and discounts sought in making purchases.)

10. On a detailed map of your community make a blue dot at the residence of each member of your church and a red dot at the place of his daily duties (work, school, etc.). Is your

church represented in all parts of your community? If not, why not? How can it become a more effective witness for Jesus Christ in mundane economic, political, and social affairs?

RECOMMENDED READING

Grimes, Howard, *The Church Redemptive.* New York: Abingdon Press, 1958. A discussion of the importance of the church in the day-by-day existence of the Christian.

Gustafson, James M., *Treasure in Earthen Vessels.* New York: Harper and Row, 1961. A stimulating discussion of the church as a human community.

Moberg, David O., *The Church as a Social Institution.* Englewood Cliffs, N. J.: Prentice-Hall, 1962. A textbook surveying the sociology of contemporary American religion.

Raines, Robert A., *New Life in the Church.* New York: Harper and Row, 1961. A discussion of the role of small "Koinonia" groups within the church in conversion, Christian growth, and witnessing.

Webber, George W., *God's Colony in Man's World.* New York: Abingdon Press, 1960. Observations on the life and mission of the Christian church which grow out of experiences in the East Harlem Protestant Parish.

Wilmore, Gayraud S., *The Secular Relevance of the Church.* Philadelphia: Westminster Press, 1962. Written to help laymen think theologically about difficult problems of society.

Winter, Gibson, *The Suburban Captivity of the Churches.* Garden City, N. Y.: Doubleday, 1961. A critique of contemporary American Protestantism.

PART III:

SOCIETY'S NEED FOR CHRISTIAN SOCIAL CONCERN

Chapter 4

Contemporary Social Problems

Hereby perceive we the love of God, because he laid down his life for us: and we ought to lay down our lives for the brethren.

But whoso hath this world's good, and seeth his brother have need, and shutteth up his bowels of compassion from him, how dwelleth the love of God in him?

My little children, let us not love in word, neither in tongue; but in deed and in truth (I John 3:16-18).

Thus speaketh the Lord of hosts, saying, Execute true judgment, and shew mercy and compassions every man to his brother:

And oppress not the widow, nor the fatherless, the stranger, nor the poor; and let none of you imagine evil against his brother in your heart (Zech. 7:9-10).

Ever since Adam and Eve ate of the forbidden fruit in the Garden of Eden, man has been plagued by social problems. The Bible presents a sorry record of murder, drunkenness, war, corrupt government, false religious leaders, lying, theft, sexual immorality, slavery, exploitation of the poor and weak, injustice, and a host of other problems which reflect the failure of men to love their neighbors. Social problems are not new!

Many if not all of God's blessings to mankind can be transformed into a curse. The great productivity of modern industry is accompanied by problems of smog, water pollution, and depletion of natural resources. Abundant food supplies are accompanied by problems of gluttony and obesity, with premature death to the person who has an oversupply of cholesterol. Nuclear energy is exploited for war-related purposes. The blessing of physical survival to old age is accompanied by problems of economic, social, and psychological adjustment of the aged and the failure of society to provide worthwhile roles for them. God's gift of sex is perverted in numerous ways. The benefits of family life are twisted into problems of family relationships, divorce, and marital maladjustment. The conquest of infant mortality through great advances in sanitation and medicine is accompanied by the specter of a world population explosion and its accompaniments of malnutrition, starvation, and unemployment. The greed and selfishness of men thus transmute many of God's blessings, making evils come from them. Man's sinfulness is manifested by and reflected in social problems.

Christian social concern is directed primarily toward social problems. Love leads to efforts to help other men physically, materially, and socially as well as spiritually. It extends to the prevention, alleviation, and elimination of social problems as well as to the treatment of persons who suffer, for social problems are the problems of persons.

Social Problems Are Personal

Every problem situation in society and hence in the world is in the final analysis a problem of individual persons. It is very easy to consider the problems of society in an abstract manner, forgetting that all social problems are intensely *personal* problems for those who are their victims. For instance, the technological unemployment which results from automation in coal and iron mines contributes directly to the loss of jobs by individual miners. It causes suffering for themselves and their families. It harms the businessmen they patronize, the churches and charities they normally support, and the entire community of which they are a part. Loss of employment causes reduced buying power. This in turn indirectly contributes to the loss of jobs by other people who are involved in the production of goods which would have been purchased had employment continued. Similarly, radioactive fallout may seem to be a remote problem of international relationships, but for the family of the infant that has died as a result of atmospheric contamination it is an intensely grievous and heart-rending tragedy.

Problems pertinent to the economic order, such as poverty, the abuse of credit, bankruptcy, automation, unemployment due to strikes and lockouts, migratory agricultural labor, child labor, underemployment (low-income or part-time work which forces people to live on a marginal economic level), fluctuations of the business cycle, inflation, costs of illness, and retirement-pension problems all have direct personal implications for many people. Indirectly they affect all people, not only those in the nation immediately involved but virtually everyone on the face of the earth.

Problems of community relationships like Sunday observance, racial segregation, housing discrimination, juvenile delinquency, white-collar crime (violation of the law in the course of a legitimate business, professional, or occupational role), other crimes, transiency, difficulties of recreational services and facilities, and mental illness all affect individual persons and their families.

Problems of national and international affairs include those of civil liberties, political corruption, graft, revolution, disarmament, war, conscription, migration, and overpopulation of the world or of specific regions within it. Each of these has far-reaching implications for people as individuals.

The problems related to marriage and family life, such as divorce, marital separation, family discord, parent-child conflict, infant mortality, orphans, dependent children, maternal mortality, old age, widowhood, desertion, hasty marriage, elopement, black-market and gray-market baby adoptions, illegitimacy, mental retardation, racial and religious intermarriage, malnutrition, mental illness, physical and psychosomatic illness, mercy killing, and disability have a very direct effect upon the lives of all persons involved.

Patterns of conflict in society represented by anti-Semitism, racial struggles, Protestant-Catholic conflicts, and other forms of intergroup friction have resulted in many lynchings and riots. Bloodshed and personal suffering result from these for large numbers of people. Unwholesome social patterns of self-perpetuating hatred are linked with discrimination against minority groups. These lead to personal suffering by minority persons which is incomprehensible to members of majority groups.

Many personal problems also have profound social implications.

They therefore are social problems, the problems of society. They often call for welfare assistance of one type or another for preventive, corrective, or ameliorative purposes. They reach into the innermost recesses of community and family life. These problems of a more narrowly personal kind include illness, deafness, blindness, accidents, suicide, venereal disease, homosexuality, and pornography, as well as drug addiction and prostitution.

The dedicated Christian cannot remain indifferent to social problems. They have far-reaching implications for all of society and thus for every person within society. The sense of purposelessness, restlessness, and anxiety which is so evident among people from all levels of life overlaps with and often is a result of these other problems. For example, feelings of personal rejection in old age are linked with the failure of society in general to provide meaningful roles for the aged. Personal difficulties in social relationships arise when a capable person is forced against his will to retire prematurely from work simply because he has reached a compulsory retirement age. The juvenile school dropout may similarly be seeking an acceptable role in society when he engages in delinquent behavior.

Problems of family life affect many more persons than the individual who appears most directly to be their victim. The illness of a mother reflects upon the life of her husband and all of his occupational, recreational, and other social relationships as well as his activities within the home. It affects the lives of the children and often creates problems of child care during the day when the husband is at work. The problems associated with such illness are reflected in some communities in competition to get a hospital bed when there are more patients than facilities available to meet their needs. The shortage of medical personnel in many rural communities also becomes a personal problem when a person in need of treatment cannot receive it because it is unavailable. Many problems are reinforced in a circular pattern, by which the effect of a cause in turn becomes a further cause of the problem condition.

Basic Principles About Social Problems

Knowledge, theories, and insights from the various social sciences can help Christians respond realistically to the complex problems of social relationships. Many principles which come from scientific research on social problems can help Christians to love their neighbors as they love themselves. Some of these deal with the causes, others with the effects, and still others with proposed solutions to social problems. A few examples of these principles and some of their Christian implications follow.

Causes. Every social problem has many causes. The immediate causes are complex and frequently unknown or not fully known. Conditions and circumstances of the present and past are woven together in a complex network or configuration of causes.

The causes of a problem are an integral part of the total society, so they cannot be understood apart from understanding this total society. Many of the problems that lead to welfare needs, for example, have their source in increasingly high educational requirements for jobs as they become more technical. People with less than a high-school education are much more likely to be without work than those who have completed high school. But low educational attainment is itself a product of low aspirations, poor teaching that discourages some persons from completing school, discrimination that segregates members of minority groups into certain schools which may be at great time/cost distance from their residences and which typically have been inferior in quality, problems of poverty in the home which push children out to work at an early age or hinder them from going on to college, the feeling of minorities that no matter how much education they get, they will at best be railway porters or janitors, and other conditions. Each social problem thus contributes to others. All are interrelated. A "vicious circle" of causation prevails.

Some of the causes of a specific problem may be conditions that are basically desirable. Men cannot be sure that they know all the causes, and causes themselves are effects of other causes. A recognition of these principles will prevent us from promoting simplistic proposals for social action.

The increase in divorce which has occurred in this century, for example, is in part a result of the economic emancipation of women, their desire as a result of increased education to have a greater part in family decisions, the increasing freedom of the individual from the social controls of his neighborhood and family, the urbanization of our population, industrialization, the decline of religious sanctions upon individual and family behavior, and an emphasis on romantic love. Americans generally would not wish to give up these developments, so they will continue to have the resulting problems. Social changes which most of us judge to be good frequently bring about results which we deem evil.

Similarly, the invention of the automobile has had many wholesome results, but it also has some effects that most Christians would call evil. It has made it easier for youth to engage in immoral behavior, for criminals to elude law enforcement agencies, and for many people to attempt to keep ahead of the Joneses through trying to have a better automobile than theirs.

Sin as a Cause. From a theological perspective, sin is the ultimate source of all social problems. In the immediate and contemporary sense, however, the causes are often too complex to attribute directly to sin. The victims of social problems are not necessarily worse sinners than others. All have sinned and come short of God's glory; none is fully righteous (Rom. 3:9-23). This was part of the lesson which Jesus taught His disciples when He told them about the suffering of the Galileans at the hand of Pilate and the eighteen upon whom the tower in Siloam fell (Luke 13:1-5). It also was one of the lessons linked with the healing of the man born blind (John 9:1-3). While sin does cause many, perhaps all, social problems, it is not always the sin of the *victims* which directly brings about their plight.

This is obvious in such events as the "Christmas present" received in 1963 by about 8,800 employees of the Studebaker plant in South Bend, Indiana. The factory was shut down, leaving about one out of every five workers in the entire labor force of the community without a job. In addition, the Bendix Corporation in the same city laid off four hundred workers. The diligence, honesty, efficiency, spirituality, and other virtues of individual workers were to no avail; excellent workmen and faithful Christians found themselves without employment.

Many social problems are results of natural catastrophes like floods, earthquakes, tornadoes, and volcanic eruptions. Others are caused by natural processes of aging or by diseases and defects for which man has not yet found an effective preventive or control. For example, approximately three out of every hundred infants is mentally deficient; these retarded children are born into families from all levels of social class, education, income, and occupation. They are born into the homes of sincere Christians as well as into those of nominal church members, unbelievers, and agnostics.

The very fact of modern large-scale social organization and technological invention contributes to social problems which are byproducts of basic cultural patterns like the impersonal bureaucratic forms of social organization that dominate large-scale organizations. It is difficult to see a direct link between such problems and sin, although, as in the case of poor water-conservation practices, it might be possible to trace at least a part of the causal pattern to the sinful deeds of exploiting lumber barons, mining corporations, or farmers.

Furthermore, even the moral man resides in a society which has incorporated immoral attitudes, customs, and practices into its basic institutions. Illustrations include the injustices of racial discrimination and segregation in both the South and North, the self-seeking greed that lies at the heart of much political action by all political parties, the covetous grasping for wealth that is incorporated into much business endeavor, the struggle for status and bigger incomes by the professional societies and labor unions of all occupations, the isolationist perspective toward international relations that seeks to increase a nation's own wealth and give underdeveloped peoples no aid in developing their potential resources, the mentality of hate which justifies killing even innocent women and children in warfare, the "let the buyer beware" perspective in business, the blessing placed upon abuses of alcohol by "office parties" and government-operated taverns and liquor stores, and the diligent search by corporations and sometimes even churches for loopholes in the law which permit legal violations of its spirit and intent. All too often we allow and even "bless" actions by a group of people which we would strongly condemn in the individual.

In addition, men have incorporated into their patterns of personal life a number of perspectives which encourage violation of the law as well as of moral principles. This becomes evident especially in connection with the moral training of children.

Children learn more by what they see than by what they are told. They are told to be honest, but they notice parents who falsely represent the child's age in order to save a bus fare.

They are taught that success in educational and occupational life is all-important even if getting ahead may be at the expense of a competitor. They are taught that success is measured in material terms; in practice, some have said, America's god is the "almighty dollar." They are encouraged to resist rules and regulations as if they are unnecessary red tape. When the child imitates adults, he often gets into trouble and is treated as a juvenile delinquent.

Resistance to obeying city ordinances which are passed for the health and safety of the public has been praised in some church circles as "keeping Caesar out of God's business." Violation of traffic laws is considered praiseworthy as long as one does not get a ticket. "No Smoking" and "Keep Off the Grass" signs are ignored in a wide variety of transportation facilities, institutions, businesses, and other semipublic places. Many people use their belief that "everybody has a racket" to justify their own cheating, lying, overcharging, unnecessary charges, and other dishonesties.

The impersonality of a large, urban, industrialized society adds to the problems of morality. The high degree of mobility of people and the wide variety of moral perspectives increase the difficulties of gaining moral consensus and enforcing moral standards, especially those that deal with borderline issues.

Christians should abandon simple moralistic interpretations which always attribute people's involvement in social problems to their personal acts of sin. Some of these problems have natural causes over which man has no control. Some are the results of deeds committed with good intentions. Some are effects of kind, moral behavior which also produced desirable goods and services. Only a portion are the direct effect of the victims' personal sin. The guilt for sin is widespread. It is shared by all or nearly all who are members of a society, not by the victims of social problems alone.

Sin is widely diffused throughout all of society. It often wears the disguise of moral conduct. It is not limited to those who obviously suffer. In many instances they are more innocent than the prosperous who seem on the surface to be without guile but inwardly and actually may be like ravenous wolves shedding blood and destroying lives for dishonest gain (Ezek. 22:

27). The righteous often wonder why many wicked people become prosperous and wealthy (see Psalms 73 and 94).

Effects. Social problems do not affect all persons in the same way. Some people literally subsist on the suffering of others. Auto-body repair men live on the crashes and dents of others' automobiles. Police, insurance agents, lawyers, social workers, psychiatrists, medical doctors, chaplains, and many other people devote nearly all of their working time to either the treatment or the prevention of social problems.

Until relatively recently in world history, unemployment has been a "blessing" to large employers. They have been able in periods of unemployment to hire laborers at greatly reduced wages and thus to make greater profits. Labor unions and government controls have largely stopped such abuses, but they demonstrate that what one group sees as a problem may not be recognized as a problem at all by people who live under different circumstances.

A city may have a housing shortage even when hundreds of homes for sale or rent are advertised in the daily newspapers. How can this be? The housing shortage is suffered by people in the lowest one-third to one-half of the social class structure. For the wealthy there is never a housing shortage. Furthermore, some slum landlords build up personal wealth and prosperity in part because their tenants live in misery.[1]

Critics of the contemporary Christian church condemn its flight to the suburbs. Suburban people must have churches, so there is nothing wrong with building churches in the suburbs. There is, however, a danger that accompanies the movement of middle- and upper-class church members into the suburbs. Most of the people who live in daily misery because they are poor, aged, disabled, members of minority races, undereducated, unskilled, illiterate, or of borderline mentality live in blighted and slum areas of the inner city or in relatively isolated rural areas. Christians in prosperous suburban communities are not likely to notice the misery of many of their fellow men. Since lower class and colored people are out of sight, they are apt to be out of mind. The economically prosperous Christian to whom they are

---

[1] For a vivid description of one such case, see William Manchester, "The Life and Times of a Slum Landlord," *The Reporter*, XV (Nov. 15, 1956), 24-26.

out of sight and out of mind is not likely to realize that, by ignoring their plight, he is violating the scriptural command to love his neighbor as himself. If anyone has material goods and sees his brother have need but closes his heart against him, does God's love abide in him? (I John 3:17).

It is impossible for people to escape the effects of many social problems by their own efforts. The individual is powerless to protect himself by personal efforts alone against many kinds of crime, fires, unemployment, disease epidemics, mental illness, racial discrimination, war, and accidents. Even the person who vows that he will never enter an airplane or automobile because of the danger of being involved in an accident may become a victim if an airplane or automobile crashes into his home or swoops down upon him as he walks along a city street or country road.

Furthermore, every person is affected by taxation for government services related to social problems. Nobody lives to himself (Rom. 14:7); this is reflected in the ways in which men work together to cope with social problems, often through governmental action which is supported through various forms of taxation. Social welfare services are an integral part of modern society. They impinge upon the lives of all people at many points and in diverse ways.

Most Americans are covered by the numerous provisions of the Social Security Act and are making weekly, monthly, or quarterly payments into its programs of "social insurance." Taxes to the local, state, and federal governments are used, in part, to provide correctional and welfare services for persons involved in many kinds of social problems. Voluntary organizations fighting specific types of social problems make numerous charity appeals to the average citizen. Persons with whom one associates may become recipients of welfare services. One may himself use the specialized services of a social worker just as he uses the services of a medical doctor, lawyer, or pastoral counselor.

The effects of social problems thus flow to all. They are not limited to economically poor people nor to those who experience personal disorganization or social pathology in the narrow and direct sense of those concepts. Everybody is influenced by them.

Solutions. Since individuals cannot escape the impact of many social problems through their own efforts, they are compelled to cooperate with others to fight social problems and their effects. This collective action takes many forms.

Private insurance programs and private welfare agencies emerged in the modern world to help people cope with economic and other effects of social problems. (Earlier forms of neighborliness like barn raisings, husking bees, and work parties also were a type of "insurance.") Government regulation of trade and commerce, mass communications, water supply, sewage, and such matters as wages, child labor, and maternal health are other forms of dealing cooperatively with certain kinds of social problems. When private voluntary agencies fail to solve overwhelming social problems, people work through government because all people share the benefits of treating them, and the costs can be widely distributed.

Social legislation is not a new phenomenon in America. It goes back to the very founding of the United States of America, preceding the rise of Marxist socialism by three-quarters of a century. Police services, armies, navies, and other forms of general defense against outside enemies and protection from internal social problems also involve government action to deal with areas of social concern. Hence governmental involvement in social problems goes back to the very establishment of government among mankind.

People who oppose "welfare legislation" on the basis that it is "creeping socialism" usually fail to understand that the very nature of government demands promoting the welfare of the people. The fact was recognized in the Preamble to the Constitution of the United States, which reads as follows:

> We, the people of the United States, in order to form a more perfect Union, establish justice, insure domestic tranquility, provide for the common defence, *promote the general welfare,* and secure the blessings of liberty to ourselves and our posterity, do ordain and establish this Constitution for the United States of America. (Italics added.)

It is absolutely essential, both from the viewpoint of prevention and treatment, for people to work together to cope with social problems. Democratic government upholds the welfare of individual persons. In contrast to authoritarian states which believe that the individual exists for the welfare of the state,

71

concern for the individual person predominates in democracies. Of course, abuses of governmental authority and power must always be guarded against. Members of every organization should be alert to prevent means instituted for valid ends from becoming self-justifying ends in themselves.

Conditions of the modern world have introduced an increasing need to contend with social problems on the national and international level. Because people can move readily from one country, state, and nation to another, infectious diseases cannot be controlled on a purely local level. The same is true of such problems as war, radioactive fallout, and even education.

If a child's education in a rural school of Alabama, Alaska, Arkansas, North Dakota, or West Virginia is inferior in terms of the demands of the modern world, the areas to which these children later move when they seek work in metropolitan industries and business will suffer from their deficiencies. Even in low-status positions, if a person cannot read his job instructions and cannot participate intelligently in constructive community organizations, including the church, he seriously hampers both himself and society at large. The defects of an educational system in one state thus become the concern of industry and community leadership in other states.

Local problems have thus become state problems; state problems have developed into national problems, and national problems are increasingly international in scope. When the expansion of government services meets human needs, the change promotes human dignity and freedom.

The interdependence of all mankind is more and more apparent in the social institutions of every nation. As commerce between the nations increases, other kinds of involvement also increase. Even the movement of Christian missionaries into a foreign nation brings with it political implications, for the home government exercises political concern over the welfare of its citizens. Because of the growing interdependence of all people, the United Nations has begun investigations of civil liberties and human rights. Moreover, it continues to deal with problems of health, population pressures, education, narcotics, agricultural production, and a host of other welfare-related topics which go far beyond its direct concern for international peace.

Results of Solutions. Solutions to social problems are seldom as completely wholesome as their proponents had claimed. Neither are their effects as undesirable as their opponents had feared. When national prohibition was introduced, for example, statements made by many churchmen implied that nearly all problems of society would be resolved or sharply reduced as a result. Evangelist Billy Sunday, for instance, proclaimed:

> The reign of tears is over. The slums will soon be only a memory. We will turn our prisons into factories and our jails into storehouses and corncribs. Men will walk upright now, women will smile, and the children will laugh. Hell will be forever for rent.[2]

Before the decade was over, the wets were attributing all the evils of society to prohibition, using the same techniques as the drys had before them.

Some social problems were alleviated by national prohibition, but others were accentuated. The Kefauver crime investigating committee revealed that new types of criminal gangs developed to provide "respectable citizens" with the goods and services they desired. Organized crime grew rapidly; much of the strength of syndicate crime, racketeering labor unions, and gambling businesses to this very day can be traced back to the prohibition era.[3] People who were law-abiders became law-violators; drinking became the "smart" thing to do. Against such pressures effective police enforcement of the law was impossible.

Solutions to social problems may contradict values that we cherish highly. We cannot often have our cake and eat it, too! For example, more people have been killed in automobile accidents in the United States than the total number killed in all war casualties of the nation. Yet few are eager to eliminate automobiles! The "perfect solution" for divorce would be to get rid of marriage. With no marriages, there could be no divorce. But society would crumble if that were done!

A popular "solution" for juvenile deliquency holds that when

2 Quoted by Andrew Sinclair, *Era of Excess* (New York: Harper and Row, Colophon ed., 1964), p. 248.

3 Russell R. Dynes, *et al., Social Problems: Dissensus and Deviation in an Industrial Society* (New York: Oxford University Press, 1964), pp. 559-560. As Sinclair said, "The worst hang-over of prohibition in the United States has been the criminal control of large areas of American business and labor" (*op. cit.,* p. 415).

a child becomes delinquent, his father is at fault and should be punished by a workhouse or prison sentence. If this were done, parental control over the juvenile would be removed for the duration of the sentence. The father's income during the sentence would be lost, and he might even find himself without a job upon his return to society. To meet family needs, his lost income would have to be replaced by other resources during his absence. These usually would be social welfare funds, so taxes would increase. During his sentence the father would build up resentment against his child, which in turn might so damage their relationship that the child would eventually become still more delinquent.[4]

Sources of Solutions. The basic values to guide social action cannot come from science, although the sciences may help to clarify them and especially to indicate their implications. The values applied in the sciences are always derived from other sources in a society, and ultimately their source *should* be religion.

As scientists and other leaders increasingly recognize this fact, the Christian encounters more and more occasions for exercising a social witness. Grasping such opportunities wisely will greatly advance the cause of Jesus Christ. But if Christians promote unrealistic and fanciful "solutions" to social problems, ignore the findings of scientific research, or are carried away into other unwise proposals, they will play directly into the hands of the enemies of the gospel and do more harm than good.

Some Implications

Since all social problems are also personal problems, treating them is a form of "personal aid." This is true even when it takes the form of political action or support of large-scale organizations and movements aimed at bringing about basic social

---

4 Punishing the parent for his child's delinquency also rests upon a logical error or deterministic fallacy. If the child is not at fault, neither is the parent, who is believed to be the source of the delinquency, for the parent's failure must in turn be a product of *his* parents' failure to rear him properly. But why, then, did the grandparents fail? Because of their parents! And so we move back until we reach the Garden of Eden! Perhaps this is related to the concept of "original sin" or to certain disputed interpretations of Exodus 20:5; 34:7; Numbers 14:18; and Deuteronomy 5:9.

reforms. Combating social problems is not helping "society" in an abstract and impractical sense. It is helping persons, even if the help is offered professionally and somewhat impersonally.

Often, in fact, personal help is *more* effective when provided through impersonal agencies and by the effecting of general social changes than when it is given directly. A good job retraining program is more valuable than a basket of groceries for the man who is technologically unemployed. Christians are sometimes like the people who try to control flies by using only fly swatters and sticky tape. Their job is never done. But if the flies can be stopped from breeding, fly swatters are seldom needed. Social action is often more effective than social welfare! (This, of course, does not deny that there is a great need for the "personal touch" in most areas of human need. This will be clarified in later chapters, especially Chapter 9.)

The church ought to provide moral guidance in the name of God for all of society. When it remains silent on the admittedly difficult but practical issues which pertain to the causes, effects, and solutions of social problems, it renounces its claim that it ministers to "the whole man." Such a ministry must include a concern for material and physical needs as well as for those which are "spiritual" in the narrow sense of that term. Haphazard, uncoordinated programs of action against occasional specific evils will not provide a community or nation with the kind of comprehensive planning that it needs. Neither will careful plans by isolated pastors, laymen, or congregations. Cooperative effort within and between denominations and between churches and other social institutions is increasingly required as man's interdependence multiplies with the technological, economic, political, and social changes of a world in flux.

The church may focus primarily upon the moral aspects of social problems, but its interpretations will have many direct and indirect implications for action. A Christian theology of leisure is greatly needed to influence individual and social adjustments to the growth of leisure time in the modern world. Questions about the morality of the concentration of wealth and income in the hands of relatively few people are significantly related to programs of social legislation and taxation. Clarification of the nature of man in an automated era in which machines push the push buttons may influence certain aspects of technological progress. The moral issues pertaining to injuries and deaths from highway accidents need careful attention in the church. Whether men should be moved to jobs or jobs to men when technology shifts work patterns is not a purely technological question, for it concerns such moral matters as the disruption of family life and community ties. Many such technical subjects are heavily loaded with ethical and religious significance. Realistic appraisal of such topics is therefore essential. Such appraisal must recognize the perspectives of both the social sciences and Christian values in order to be fruitful.

Since the implications of social problems for the Christian are a major focus of this entire book, further elaboration will be left to later chapters.

SUGGESTIONS FOR DISCUSSION AND STUDY

1. Why are many Christians poor and many of the prosperous wicked? How should Christians respond to the way in which God blesses the unrighteous? (See Psalms 73 and 94.) Is this related in any way to Jesus' instruction, "Judge not, that ye be not judged" (Matt. 7:1)?

2. Jesus said that "ye have the poor always with you" (Matt. 26:11). Did He mean that it is no use trying to eliminate poverty? Are there poor people in your community? Who are they? What are their living conditions? What are the causes of their problems?

3. Do any people in your community believe that youth is "going to the dogs"? Why? How do present attitudes to this subject compare with those of a generation ago?

4. Think of any one major social problem of modern society. What conditions, historical and otherwise, have led to the present problem condition? Is the problem an inevitable result of basically desirable changes?

5. How much control do you have over your own social environment? (Consider your own work, other personal activities, and community, national, and international affairs and agencies which are in any way related to you.)

6. Read the reference to Niebuhr given below. In what ways

are you and your Christian friends personally involved in social sins? What ought Christians to do about this problem? What can they do?

7. Identify some forms of sinfulness that are typically disguised as moral or at least acceptable conduct in your community. (The reference to Barron will help.) How do respectable citizens contribute to the problems of crime and delinquency? How can Christians refrain from being squeezed into the mold of their society?

8. Select a specific social problem which has been prevalent throughout history. Skim through the Bible and list all references to it which you can locate. Are common elements present in the scriptural record and in experiences with it today? Has the attitude of God's people toward it changed down through the centuries?

9. What special problems do members of minority groups (Negroes, Jews, American Indians, Puerto Ricans, Orientals, etc.) face in your community? Consider job-hunting, haircuts, buying a home, renting a hotel room, registering to vote, eating in restaurants, sending a child to school, attending concerts, swimming, and seeking a church home. Discuss this question with several members of minority groups in your community. How do their perspectives on this topic differ from those of white middle-class Protestants? Why?

10. Identify several proposed solutions to a contemporary social problem. Summarize the claims of proponents of each solution and the counterarguments of its opponents. Are any of the ideas they express directly contradictory? What are their sources? How many of the arguments are based upon clear facts, and how many represent vague opinions? What hidden assumptions underlie the perspectives? Do other social problems help to explain the contrasting views? What tests can be applied to determine which viewpoint is the most consistent with facts and with Christian values?

RECOMMENDED READING

Barron, Milton L., "The Delinquent Culture of American Society," Chapter 12 in *The Juvenile in Delinquent Society*. New York: Alfred A. Knopf, 1952. A survey of social forces inherent in the culture of the American people which impel youth to delinquency.

Dynes, Russell R., *et al.*, *Social Problems: Dissensus and Deviation in an Industrial Society*. New York: Oxford University Press, 1964. One of several excellent college textbooks surveying American social problems.

Kenrick, Bruce, *Come Out the Wilderness*. New York: Harper and Row, 1962. The story of the East Harlem Protestant Parish; includes vivid description of the social problems which reinforce each other in Harlem, New York City.

McGee, Reece, *Social Disorganization in America*. San Francisco: Chandler, 1962. A paperback interpretation and survey of social problems.

Niebuhr, Reinhold, *Moral Man and Immoral Society*. New York: Scribner's, 1932. A study in ethics and politics which notes a sharp distinction between the moral behavior of individuals and the ethics of national, racial, economic, or other social groups to which they belong.

Schorr, Alvin L., *Slums and Social Insecurity*. Washington, D. C.: U.S. Government Printing Office, 1963 (Social Security Adm., HEW). A summary of social science studies of the relationships between substandard housing and continuous poverty in the U.S.

PART IV:

IMPLEMENTING CHRISTIAN SOCIAL CONCERN

Chapter 5

The Church and Social Concern

He that hath an ear, let him hear what the Spirit saith unto the churches (Rev. 3:22).
Now unto him that is able to do exceeding abundantly above all that we ask or think, according to the power that worketh in us,
Unto him be glory in the church by Christ Jesus throughout all ages, world without end. Amen (Eph. 3:20-21).

WE HAVE SEEN THAT THE CHURCH IS PEOPLE — THE PEOPLE OF God entrusted with duties of evangelism, education, service, and prophecy. All of these duties are summed up in the Great Commission of Jesus Christ. He gave His disciples a missionary task of going, preaching, baptizing, and teaching (Matt. 28:18-20; Acts 1:8). If Christ's will is to be done, every Christian must possess a sincere and deep social passion, for a church is not likely to be nobler than its members. Neglecting to accept and implement social responsibility will weaken other aspects of a church's mission.

Carrying the gospel into all the world means carrying it into every nook and cranny of our own society as well as into foreign nations. Christian social concern is one of the means by which the gospel is extended into community affairs as well as personal lives. Implementing Christian social concern is thus one form of evangelism. It is clearly a part of God's revealed will, as we noted in Chapters 1, 2, and 3.

Types of Christian Social Concern

Social concern can be divided into two chief categories. *Social welfare* consists of ministries to help the victims of

81

personal and social problems. It aims at removing or alleviating their suffering by direct treatment of themselves and their environmental circumstances. Chapter 6 deals with welfare programs of churches, and Chapter 9 suggests many types of volunteer services to help meet welfare needs. Chapters 7 and 8 also include suggestions directly related to social welfare.

Social action has the goal of changing or reforming basic conditions in society which cause human need. It aims at eliminating the sources of human suffering or, if this is impossible, alleviating the specific conditions which cause it. Much of Chapter 7 and parts of Chapter 8 focus upon this aspect of Christian service.

Underlying both social welfare and social action is a *social philosophy*, an interpretation of man's social relationships in terms of ultimate values. The philosophy may not be expressed in systematic written form, but it is an orientation which gives direction to all aspects of behavior. It consists of a set of values, norms, criteria for action, ideas of right and wrong, standards of good and bad, and the like, which guide human thought and actions.

The Christian's philosophy of personal life and involvement in society ought to be based upon Scripture. This book is basically an effort to express a Christian philosophy of social concern that is consistent with evangelical Christian theology, the realities of the contemporary world, and the organizational structure and administrative patterns of operation of typical Protestant churches. The practical implications of such a philosophy are the chief concern of Part IV.

In this chapter we will survey some patterns of Christian social concern, principles for church service, and precautions related to dangers which are linked with such service.

Patterns of Christian Social Concern

Everything done by the church as an organization and as a people scattered throughout society has implications for Christian social concern. Some of the general activities of a church which provide a foundation for social welfare and social action will be presented here.

Prevention. A primary social function of the church is the prevention of evil. When Sunday school promoters appeal to parents to give their children a Christian education so that they will not become juvenile delinquents, they testify indirectly to the preventive work of the church. Religious education alone does not always prevent delinquent behavior, but it does have a generally wholesome effect on human conduct.

The church's evangelism also helps to prevent social problems. It is extremely difficult to persuade a person to want to do good and show a concern for others, that is, to keep the "Golden Rule" (Matt. 7:12). Christian commitment, however, influences basic human motivations (Matt. 15:16-20; Gal. 5:16-24; etc.). When people accept Christ as their Saviour and Lord, they receive new self-images. These are very significant in decisions that pattern one's behavior. Christians conceive of themselves as children of God, new creatures in Christ, saints, a royal priesthood, a holy nation, God's own unique ("peculiar") people, citizens of the Kingdom of God (John 1:12; Acts 11:26; Rom. 1:7; I Cor. 1:2; II Cor. 5:17; Col. 1:12-13; I Pet. 2:9; I John 3:1-2; etc.). What a person thinks himself to be in his own mind he rapidly becomes in fact.

Christian self-images and the peace of being rightly related to God and man prevent many mental disorders, psychosomatic illnesses, and problems of interpersonal relationships. While the "peace of mind" cult goes too far in its claims at several points, the truth at its base should not be ignored. The "spiritual" ministry of the church, even in the most narrow sense of that term, helps to prevent many problems of persons, families, other social groups, and society as a whole.

Therapy. The church's conventional ministry also has a therapeutic effect. As it prevents and ameliorates some problems, it helps to cure others. One of the greatest difficulties in the treatment of alcoholics, confirmed criminals, and people with marital problems lies in giving them a desire strong enough to change their way of life. The testimonies of thousands witness to the therapeutic changes that result from a genuine conversion to Jesus Christ.

Fellowship of Christians with one another has therapeutic value for victims of social problems. Social science research and the experiences of counselors are making it increasingly clear that the sharing of insights and experiences in small groups

83

is one of the most effective forms of treatment for many types of family, personal, and other problems. This has always been the testimony of Christianity. Fellowship in worship, service, suffering, and witnessing are so prominent in the New Testament that several Christian groups prefer to be known as a "fellowship" rather than as an organization or denomination. (See Acts 2:42; I Cor. 1:9; II Cor. 6:14; 8:23; Phil. 2:1-2; 3:10; I John 1:3, 6-7.)

Accepting a person who has problems into an open, non-judgmental group has a powerful healing effect. The church that lacks "social fellowship" activities is denying its members and friends one of the most important sources of help in the prevention and treatment of personal and social problems.

Social Action. Although the church has a redemptive influence on society even when it focuses on only evangelism and "personal" needs, it must also be concerned for modification of the social structure. Otherwise social pressures may become so great that the seed which sprouts to life is choked and overcome by cares and pressures of this world (Mark 4:1-20).

A truly Christian concern for people who have been caught by grievous social problems will lead eventually to a concern for preventing the problems. Christians have sometimes been criticized for their eagerness to help victims of problems while refusing to help prevent similar future suffering caused by the same conditions. We must attempt to extinguish the destructive flames of social problems, but we must also cut off the fuel which is feeding those flames. In other words, a realistic concern for human distress will lead eventually to social action to prevent it.

It is not right to preach about social evils if we refuse to do what we can to overcome them. If we engage only in a fallacious negativistic program, we are in effect cutting out and throwing away significant portions of the Bible by ignoring their implications for our own personal and group action. Constructive criticism by the church is necessary if it is to be the conscience of society. Like salt, or leaven, or a mustard seed (Matt. 5:13; 13:31-33), which eventually pervades the world with the influence of its values and effects, the witness of the church in its education and by the example of its own action should permeate all of society.

Christians should establish a reputation for positive rather than purely negative social action. When they get the name of speaking only in words of protest, they are not likely to be heard. Similarly, if they are concerned only with promoting the interests of the church as an institution instead of the welfare of mankind, their appeals are likely to fall upon deaf ears. If Christians promote a positive program which supports mercy, truth, justice, love, and the good of all people, their words will be heard when they occasionally speak out against programs and policies of the community or nation which violate such principles. Chapter 7 suggests some of the ways in which a wholesome impact for Jesus Christ can be made upon the "secular" world.

Education. The educational ministries of the church also have a close relationship to social concern. Teaching the Scriptures faithfully necessitates recognition of social evils, formulation of a Christian philosophy of social concern, and guidance to Christians on how to discharge their social responsibilities as good stewards of Jesus Christ.

The preaching and teaching roles of the ministry should stimulate and support social services by the laity in their daily occupations, community relations, citizenship obligations, and volunteer service opportunities. In order to see the practical relevance of the Bible to daily life in a rapidly changing world, the church must shoulder its share of responsibility for the continuing education of adults as well as for teaching children. What people learned in high school and college ten or twenty years ago may be sadly out of date. Conclusions about the details of Christian living developed in the horse-and-buggy age may be totally irrelevant in our emerging cyber-cultural society.

The Bible will never be out of date. But some of its followers are backward. They fail to see the difference between God's Word and translations of it or between the Bible message and men's interpretations and applications of it. This prevents many Christians from recognizing it as "a light that shineth in a dark place" (II Pet. 1:19) to guide men through life. It also feeds the prejudices of agnostics and atheists.

Sometimes a system of Bible interpretation is elevated into an absolute requirement of belief. When this is done, whether the system be presented in the form of commentaries, Bible notes, or a "key to the Scriptures," the Word of God has been handled deceitfully and an idol has been erected to take the place of God Himself (see II Cor. 4:2; II Tim. 3:16-17; Tit. 1:9-16; Jas. 1:21-25; II Pet. 1:19—2:3; etc.). One of the greatest blessings of this generation is its large number of modern translations of the Bible. Even those who do not understand the original languages of the Scriptures thus have access to a wealth of clarification of their message. Christian education should always take advantage of these resources. They take the Bible out of the realm of antiquated seventeenth-century concepts and make it a relevant contemporary book.

Self-Sacrifice. The well-organized church which carefully tries to implement its social responsibility will soon recognize that human wisdom and scientific knowledge are not enough to solve social problems. A much deeper challenge to human sin and social conflict is needed. The Christian gospel with its doctrine of redemption must be demonstrated to the world.

The voluntary giving of self, the sacrifice of self-advantage on behalf of others as a result of Christ's compassion and concern for the sins and sufferings of others, is alien to the spirit of the world. It is the plus-factor of Christianity which should be held up as the ideal for human social service. This ideal is patterned after the example of Jesus Christ, who "made himself of no reputation, and took upon him the form of a servant, and was made in the likeness of men: And being found in fashion as a man, he humbled himself, and became obedient unto death, even the death of the cross" (Phil. 2:7-8).

Prayer. Because divine wisdom is needed, prayer is a significant part of the social ministry of a church. It, too, is an aspect of church action. It includes prayers of confession for past and present failures; prayers of petition for guidance in interpreting and applying the Word of God in contemporary society; prayers of intercession for men who suffer, for those who help them through public and private social welfare, and for those who try to reform the conditions that caused their trouble; prayers of thanksgiving for successful achievements; and prayers of praise to God who always gives the victory and whom the Christian knows to be the omnipotent Sovereign of the universe. Even the shut-in church member can participate in Christian service through prayer.

Christians should pray for leaders in public life, who often are lonely, socially isolated from the perspective of personal and emotional burdens. They should pray for the rulers of even antichristian nations (I Tim. 2:1-4; cf. Rom. 13:1-10). They should remember social workers, counselors, and others in the "helping professions" who at times get discouraged and wonder whether they are achieving anything worthwhile. They should pray that God will thrust them forth as laborers into that portion of His harvest field for which they are best qualified by ability and opportunity. Then they can do daily work in the knowledge that it is indeed a vocation — a task to which they have been called by God They should pray for humility in their individual and social lives. Humility will neither glory in men's wisdom nor shun it. Humility will make one ever mindful of the fact that, but for the grace of God, he himself might be the victim of numerous social problems. Humility leads one to help others in a spirit of meekness, considering one's own weakness (Gal. 6:1-5; see Matt. 7:1-5). God will honor such prayers!

Principles for Implementing Social Concern

Consistency. "Actions speak louder than words" applies to groups as well as to persons. Churches should be consistent examples of Christian virtues. If a church is inconsistent in one area of its teachings, people may believe that it cannot be trusted in any of them. Thus if a church in a bi-racial community condemns racial prejudice but has in its fellowship members of only one racial group, people will conclude that its pronouncements on race relations are merely "window dressing."

A church may emphasize the scriptural truth that in Christ there are no social class distinctions (neither "bond nor free," I Cor. 12:13; Gal. 3:28; Col. 3:11). But if it seems to cater to "important people" in the world or excludes those who are from the humbler stations of society, its example will teach that Christianity is for "respectable people" only. If a church's prestige rests on the standards of popularity or importance of the world, is it not being conformed to the world in a nonchristian way?

It is well established that the outcome of many church elections is closely related to the standards of success of society. To whatever extent this reflects qualities of leadership ability which are evident in both areas of life, this is good. To whatever extent it represents adopting worldly standards without consideration for virtues of Christian faith and character, it is an indictment against a church. Many of Jesus' most effective disciples today, as in the day when He walked the earth with the twelve, come from occupations that are lowly and despised by popular standards. The church that conforms to these standards can hardly expect to correct them.

The church should set an example to the world in its employment practices and other business dealings. It is not to the church's credit that ministers and other "full-time Christian servants" had to expect poverty and degradation during the closing years of their life until the government's social security program began to include them.

The church should also do its utmost to make sure that those who "pray on their knees on Sunday" will not "prey on their neighbors on Monday."[1] The true test of Christian discipleship is not church attendance but the influence of the gospel on daily life seven days of the week. Consistency of words and deeds characterizes those who truly are the people of God.

Adaptability. No single program of social concern fits all Christian persons and churches. Every community is different. Every individual and congregation has been given a different combination of abilities, resources, and opportunities. Denominations can provide their churches with only general suggestions as to ways of discovering and meeting needs. Churches can provide their members with only general instructions, principles, opportunities for service, and inspiration.

Flexibility. Once a program has been adopted, it must be flexible enough to change with the changing needs of a changing world. There can be no fixed "Christian status quo" in modern society. The rapid expansion of man's knowledge and the growth of his technology lead inevitably to significant changes in churches as well as in government, business, social welfare, schools, and recreation. Christians need to understand

[1] William G. Jordan, *The Kingship of Self-Control* (New York: Revell, 1899), p. 37.

these social transitions and adjust to them under the guidance of the Holy Spirit. They need to remember that the Sovereign of the universe often works in mysterious ways that will be incomprehensible to men until that day when their knowledge is made perfect.

Love. Christians should make love their aim (I Cor. 14:1) — love to neighbors as well as to brethren in Christ. All humanity is a neighbor of the Christian, so his love should extend to people the world over, not just to those in his own denomination, nation, or religion. This means a policy of "humanity first" rather than a chauvinistic emphasis on "business first," "America first," "Canada first," "NATO first," or "my own denomination first."

Love is never perfect among mankind. Most people of the world are not Christians, and even the Christian's love is imperfect. Hence it is futile to expect any society to incorporate love at its highest and noblest levels into its political and social action. But Christians should not assume that it is better to keep the status quo with all of its shortcomings than to promote change merely because that change, too, will be imperfect. Movement toward love is better than no movement at all!

Justice. This means that justice must often be the immediate goal of social action. Justice is not the *agape* love that goes the second mile, but it does provide rights and privileges to all men as equals under God. *Agape* love cannot be put into statutes and laws, for it involves the deepest motives of men's hearts. Justice does not depend upon the capacity for love of the individuals who enforce it. Man's inhumanity to man can be curbed by incorporating justice into legislative, administrative, and judicial institutions.

Justice demands that no group hold the power to exploit another. It can be established by implementing fully the human rights guaranteed in the Constitution of the United States. As justice is done toward minority groups who have previously been victims of acts of discrimination, attitudes of prejudice will gradually be modified. Prejudice is basically a reflection of pride, selfishness, and hatred. Justice hence presents a movement toward love. Even though it is not "perfect love," its implementation should be sought by the Christian.

Righteousness and justice in personal and group life are commanded repeatedly in the Bible. (Examples are Deut. 16:18-20;

Ps. 82:1-4; Prov. 1:3; 21:15; Isa. 26:7; Amos 5:7-15.) The higher ethic of love in the New Testament includes justice, but it also goes far beyond it. It holds love even for enemies as the ideal. Justice is not negated by the New Testament; it is reaffirmed and enlarged.

Justice is often the highest attainable goal in human society, for society consists of nonchristians and "carnal Christians" as well as sincere children of God. The acceptance of something less than the best (justice rather than *agape* love) does not condone sin; it simply acknowledges its presence and allows support of a realistic intermediate goal.

Competence. The church should recognize competence wherever it is found, knowing that God is the Sovereign who makes even the heathen praise Him. All who produce goods and services which in any direct or indirect way help the work of the church as either an organization or a people are aiding in the dissemination of the gospel. Most men are concerned more about the professional competence of a medical doctor needed for emergency surgery treatment than they are about his personal political or religious beliefs. The professional abilities of those who offer social services similarly should be the prime consideration in deciding to use or not to use them. In politics likewise a nonchristian legislator or administrator may merit support because his position is basically in accord with Christian values. Those who are not against Christ often are unconsciously working for Him when they do good (Mark 9:38-41).

Selectivity. No one church and none of its members can do everything worthwhile that ought to be done in the name of Jesus Christ. Choices must be made about which of many potential foreign mission fields will be entered by a given group and which it will leave untouched. In the same manner choices must be made as to which specific social services should be sponsored by a group, which volunteer services should be promoted, and which welfare programs of other agencies will be sponsored. Just as a local church has many members, each with his own responsibilities to the total Christian community, so each denomination has many local churches, each having unique functions within the denomination, depending upon the resources and opportunities God has set before them. Similarly, it is possible that each denomination has a somewhat different set of responsibilities for which it is uniquely responsible in the total Body of Christ.

Strategy. For this reason it is very important to develop an over-all strategy for implementing Christian social concern. Research to discover unmet needs of members and other people in a church's community or parish can reveal areas of need to which Christians should minister. Study of local, state, national, and international politics can clarify the positions that Christian individuals, congregations, denominations, and interdenominational organizations ought to promote among their members. Coordination of church-related efforts with those of other concerned groups can help to promote God's work. Evaluation can point to both failures and successes, enabling more efficient use of the resources of personnel, time, and money which are invested in church service. The techniques and skills of social scientists can be used effectively in such studies. Some suggestions for such research are given in Chapter 10.

Without careful planning, the Christian warfare may be concentrated on secondary battlefields while the main battlefront is lost to enemies of Christ. Rousing sermons and eloquently worded resolutions on "safe issues" will not overcome the evils which are incorporated into basic social institutions. Indeed, conformity to worldly values and deification of traditional activities are subtle forms of the enemy's infiltration.

Dangers to Avoid

In order to improve their personal and collective witness for Jesus Christ, Christians need to keep in mind principles like those in the preceding section. They also should be cautious about the pressures which bear down upon them in modern society, for many dangers lurk in the pathway of those who try to fulfill social responsibility.

Institutionalism. Organizations like persons tend to "put their best foot forward" in order to impress others by their virtue. This may lead to the disease of institutionalism. Its chief symptoms are overorganization and a perversion of goals which sets up the institution as an end in itself.

The growth of bureaucratic forms of organization is characteristic of contemporary business, education, government, social welfare, and religion. It is a necessary development in the complex modern world. But it carries with it a potential danger of letting bureaucratic growth become subversive of the basic goals of the church. Men can get so busy doing "church work" that they forget the basic work of the church.

The danger can be averted through conscientious focusing upon the basic tasks of the church. Renewed concern for human needs can bring renewal to organized groups within a church. It can provide them with goals of service beyond "fellowship and fun" and thus give them purpose and strength. Giving men's, women's, and youth groups outlets for direct Christian service in their own community and the larger world can restore their vitality and bring spiritual growth, for the greatest blessings of involvement in social service always come to the givers. For their own sake, as well as for that of neighbors in need, churches should be more involved in social action and welfare. This will overcome their introverted tendency to serve only the immediate pleasures of their own members.

Blind promotion of programs for the sake of putting trophies on the walls of institutional pride reflects a false conception of the nature and purpose of the church in the world. Like Christ, God's people will not seek their own reputation. They will not act out of selfishness and conceit (Phil. 2:3-8). Institutional strength will be a by-product of their program of service, not an ulterior motive used to deceive "prospects" for membership.

The church should not view the wholesome agencies and institutions of society as competitors draining it of people, time, and money. Rather, it should enrich them by its service; like its Lord it is in the world to serve (Matt. 20:25-28). Sometimes it will focus upon the needs of individual persons, as Jesus did when He healed the sick. At other times it will focus upon collective needs, as Jesus did when He fed the multitudes and as God does when He makes His sun to shine upon the whole earth. A wholesome balance between services to persons and activities which sweep across the needs of thousands will then prevail.

Deceit. When a church has specific standards of social service or personal piety for its membership, it should not hide these from prospective members. It is unfair to reveal these to new members only gradually, assuming that eventually they will adjust satisfactorily to membership requirements. Such a procedure may make a person feel that he has been delivered a low blow from which he cannot recover. Internal friction, dissension, and even organic division can result from this form of lying by a church fellowship.

Complacency. Once a church has established a committee on social concern or given a portion of its budget to social welfare, members may feel that they have met their social obligations fully. True Christian concern extends far beyond organizational action and financial aid. Churches and their members should take care lest such activity, which is so important as a first step, become an excuse for not taking the second. Personal involvement of many members in various types of volunteer services and social action is needed more than token activity by the church as an institution.

Misidentification. The church as an organization, of course, should never forget that it is a church. It is not a social welfare agency, although it may sponsor such agencies. It is not a political party, although it may promote certain specific political proposals. It is not a recreation center, although it may support recreational activities. It is not a fund-raising organization, although its work necessitates the raising of funds. The church should not be sidetracked from its primary responsibilities to God and man. Its aim is to promote the cause of Jesus Christ through the proclamation and application of the gospel. All church-related activities should therefore be Christ-centered.

Either-Or Thinking. The choices before men on social issues seldom represent completely black and white or right and wrong alternatives. They usually involve deciding between varying shades of gray. They are between good and better or bad and worse, not between absolute perfection on the one hand and total corruption on the other.

Christians will humbly recognize the possibility that they may err even when they act on the basis of their most solid convictions. They are likely to be found on many sides of political issues and social controversies. It is as if they were looking at a magnified photo of a newspaper; a few see the white spaces, others see the black dots, and some see both. One views a proposal as Christian, another sees it as immoral or "pagan," and still others see in it an admixture of Christian and non-christian elements.

Liberalism-Conservatism. Christian charity should be practiced toward those who do not see eye to eye on every jot and tittle with regard to social issues. Perhaps everyone is "liberal" in certain respects and "conservative" in others. Certainly none has perfect wisdom about all the affairs of this earth. We should respect the viewpoints of others, clothed in the humility that acknowledges the possibility that we, not they, might be wrong (Jas. 4:6, 10-12; I Pet. 5:5-6). To preserve our own freedom, we must protect the freedoms of others, including their freedom to make mistakes as long as they do not injure their fellow men.

The Christian ideally is both a conservative who tries to conserve all that is true, honest, just, pure, lovely, and gracious (Phil. 4:8) in society and a liberal who tries to liberate mankind by changing the conditions of society that violate those criteria of excellence. It is dangerous to change for the sake of change alone, and equally dangerous to support the status quo just because "we've always done it this way."

Christians should test all relevant evidence carefully and then hold fast what is good, abstaining from that which appears to be evil (I Thess. 5:21-22). They should distinguish between fact and opinion, between Bible teachings and interpretations of the Bible, between wholesome conservatism and obstructionist traditionalism, and between healthy modification of the current situation and revolutionary revision that would destroy good elements of the present social order along with the bad.

Extremism. "Witch-hunting" crusades may divert Christians from their primary mission. God's positive will for society will not be proclaimed when the church spends most of her energy combating "creeping socialism," the Communist menace, or other real or imagined enemies. Communists will never overthrow our government if we successfully control the social problems which allow them to gain a foothold. A positive attack on poverty, unemployment, mental illness, disease, political corruption, racial discrimination, materialism, hedonism, moral decadence, juvenile delinquency, the population explosion, injustice, and other social problems is the best way to hamper Communist propaganda. The way to overcome evil is to do good (Rom. 12:14-21).

The most dangerous "enemy within" may be the person who insists that only his own perspective on society, his own definition of freedom, or his own interpretation of democracy is correct.

Such people typically shoot their acrimonious barbs at anyone who acknowledges the faults of his society, attempts to correct them, or protests the idolatry of materialistic nationalism that sets up Americanism or another form of nationalism as the equivalent of Christianity. They often distort words by appropriating their own special meanings for them. Their threat to use militaristic power to control "dangerous minorities" may create greater risks to our freedom and do more harm to the cause of Christ than Communism and other subversive movements.

Christians should be careful not to become linked with movements and activities that will do a disservice to Christ even while they believe they are acting in His name. Before joining any movement or participating in any activity, they should conscientiously and cautiously seek God's will through investigation, prayer, the Bible, and discussion with fellow believers. The Spirit of Truth will then guide, helping them to glorify Christ in all things (John 16:13-15).

Contention. Avoid being led astray by those who create divisions and cause dissension within the church (Rom. 16:17-18; I Cor. 1:10-13; 3:3-9; Jude 16-19). It is the love of Christians for each other, not their divisions, that demonstrates Christian discipleship (John 13:35). Those who set themselves up as judges over others are weak in their faith and filled with an unjustified pride that they have the light while other Christians supposedly walk in darkness.

Crusading extremists may charge that ministers, professors, schoolteachers, politicians, a social action committee, or other Christians are Communists, socialists, modernists, or members of some hated or feared ideological group. Typically they dare not name persons and places. To do so would make them liable to prosecution under libel laws. But their disciples read personal suspicions, fears, and hatreds into the vague generalizations. Extremists seldom define their terms clearly, for if they did so, most people would see how ridiculous their charges are.

Foolish controversies and contention about most points of Christian faith and conduct should be avoided. Those who continue to be divisive after due admonition should be rejected (Tit. 3:9-11). Examination will often show that controversial issues labeled "theological" by crusaders are at root economic, social, psychological, historical, or cultural.

Political Identification. The importance of Christian unity must not be distorted into an assumption that all must agree about the political and economic issues linked with social concerns. There are honest and Christian reasons for differences of opinion about the means to promote justice and mercy in human relationships. To identify a church tightly with any one political party is apt to make that church twist the Scriptures to fit party viewpoints instead of using the Bible to correct its opinions.

The Christian needs a degree of independence from all organized agencies in order to protect his freedom to criticize constructively. If he becomes too rigidly linked with any social group, he may lose his opportunity to help correct the sins of that group. On the other hand, the most influential changes of any organization usually result from action by people who are within it. The Christian who "lets his light shine" positively will be respected when he also lets it fall upon shady practices and morally doubtful goals.

There is no perfect institution on earth. This obviously applies to governments, businesses, industries, and schools, but it applies to the church as well. Churches consist of people who have not yet attained perfection. For this reason no earthly political organization or social and economic perspective should be equated with perfect or ideal Christianity. To do so would be to sanctify that which is unholy. It would amount to a form of idolatry.

One of the most effective ways of preventing subversive linkages of the gospel with a particular political viewpoint is to bring people from many different social classes, occupations, educational levels, and ethnic backgrounds together in Christian fellowship in the same congregation. Each perspective will then tend to counterbalance the other in wholesome discussions of the Scriptures and their contemporary implications, and the gospel will not be distorted by the self-interests of any one group. All will give and receive both praise and blame. All will stir up the others to love and good works (Heb. 10:24).

Spiritualizing. Middle-class Christians tend to make biblical passages about "the poor" and "the sick" apply only figuratively to "the spiritually poor" and "the spiritually ill." This distorts the literal message of God's Word and may even contribute to a denial of the historical activity of Jesus Christ as reflected in passages like Luke 4:18-19, Matthew 8:14-17, and Matthew 9:35-38. The compassion of Jesus was shown in tangible, not merely "spiritual," ways. We who follow His example also ought to engage in tangible works of mercy and love.

Christians must not be deceived by a modern version of the ancient Manichaean heresy, which divorced spiritual from material concerns and placed hope in Christ solely in the next world. It neglected completely the claims of this life because it assumed that all material things are evil. It is very easy to slip into a pattern of "saving souls" which implies that salvation pertains only to the future life. The doctrine of the resurrection and other scriptural teachings indicate that the total person, body as well as spirit, is important in God's plan for man's salvation. The gospel is concerned with man's existence both on earth and in heaven or hell, both in this life and the next, both in the Kingdom of God on earth and in the Kingdom of Heaven which is yet to come.

Otherworldliness. The Christian is not asked to flee from the world. He is in the world and cannot escape it, no matter how hard he tries. He is related to the society around him without doing anything special about it. He shares the common fate of all mankind and should not expect exemption from its common experiences. He is a citizen of an earthly nation and has many responsibilities in his earthly society. The question is not whether or not he is in the world, but how to exercise his citizenship in it.

Just as God loved "the world" (John 3:16), the Christian is called upon to love the world. Like his Lord, the Christian who condemns the evil in the world will not reject people of the world. If he tries to step aside from social, economic, and political involvement, he will deny the power of the gospel, withdraw the "light of the world," fail to discharge his responsibilities as a citizen, and refuse to be neighbor to men who are in need.

A basic question for the Christian in regard to his relationships to the world is how his faith should apply to and modify his roles in the numerous areas of worldly involvement in which he inevitably finds himself. One of the foremost tasks of the church as a social institution is to educate, inspire, and support the church as the people of God in their daily activities in the world.

Organization for Social Concern

In the modern world it is necessary to delegate responsibility for the leadership of church activities, for otherwise the work will not be done. This is especially true of Christian social responsibility, for it is not a commonly recognized area of church work. It is therefore advisable for every church to have a board or committee specifically charged with this task.

In some congregations this work can be performed satisfactorily through the church advisory board, deacons, elders, Christian education board, or missions and benevolence committee. The problem with assigning leadership in social concerns to an existing group is that it already has routine or traditional duties which must not be neglected. Application of time and energy to other tasks may hinder it from performing new duties. As a result, social concern may remain an orphan.

Most congregations will therefore find that it is best to assign this area of the church's work to a new committee or board. It could have any of several titles. It might be labeled the committee on social ministries, social obligations, social responsibility, social concern, social service, social welfare, or social action.

This committee or board will promote coordinated action by the church and its members, making their efforts in social welfare more widespread and effective. It will express tangibly the church's concern for the welfare of people and the community. It will lead the church in services of the kind suggested throughout this book.

Duties delegated to this branch of the church would depend upon local and denominational circumstances, including the ministries of other boards and committees. Typical tasks might include these:

—Evaluating the church's status in the community and its relevance to the daily life, work, and problems of people.
—Exploring the need for new forms of social services in the community.
—Gaining support for church-related welfare projects.
—Representing the church in community welfare programs.
—Encouraging young people to consider vocations in the ministry, other helping professions, politics, and other occupations relevant to social concern.

—Helping all members to see the Christian impact of their vocational roles.

—Leading adult education courses and Bible study groups pertinent to Christian social responsibility.

—Stimulating participation in service clubs, labor unions, political parties, and other community organizations.

—Surveying church members' interests and abilities in relationship to social welfare and social action.

—Informing church members about welfare agencies in the community and their work.

—Indicating the need to support community welfare programs, both public and private, as a part of one's Christian witness.

—Recruiting and directing volunteers to help in welfare programs.

—Distributing prayer requests for specific needs of welfare agencies and social action programs.

—Calling attention to welfare-related developments in the community, state, and nation, and encouraging appropriate social action related to them.

—Cooperating with other churches and organizations to promote Christian values in community institutions and activities.

—Referring problem persons and families to community agencies that can give them help.

—Collecting money and other contributions for church-sponsored or community welfare services.

—Keeping the congregation informed of the committee's activities and its need for the active support of every member.

Conclusion

When the Holy Spirit stimulates Christian imaginations and consciences, the church will be actively involved in a program of social concern. Some of its members will be led into social welfare occupations. Some will participate in volunteer services. Others will work in social action programs through political and other channels. Still others will educate and inspire the people of God to serve Jesus Christ in their daily work.

There is a sense in which only that service which is done in specific relationship to Jesus Christ as Lord is truly done to Christ. It is costly to serve Him. The marks of the cross are essential to such service. Only by sacrificing time, wealth, and prestige, by exercising the discipline of self-denial, and by giving of oneself personally as a ministering servant will any person or church be able to face a needy world with the compassion and love of the One who laid down His life for mankind.

SUGGESTIONS FOR DISCUSSION AND STUDY

1. What can your church do to cultivate a Christlike sensitivity to and compassion for human needs?

2. How can your church overcome the tendency of every institution to focus its concern upon perpetuating itself as an organization and thus to overlook its basic reason for existence?

3. Does any limited human viewpoint unconsciously or indirectly influence the perspectives of your church and its members on such subjects as civil rights, social security, tax-supported welfare programs, government-sponsored health insurance, programs to reduce unemployment, aid to the poor, and related matters? (Think of such factors as nationality and race, occupational identification, social class, educational background, regional biases, political memberships, and organizational ties of the members.) Is your church most interested in the upper, middle, or working class of people? Why? How does this influence its education, evangelism, and social ministries?

4. Why is it unwise for a church to identify itself with any one political party?

5. Compare the messages to the seven churches in Revelation 2:1—3:22. Do the differences between them imply that there are valid variations in the responsibilities and hence in the activities of specific church congregations?

6. Which one of the types of relationships between Christ and culture described by H. Richard Niebuhr (see below) is nearest to the traditional position of your church? Which is the most consistent with a truly Christian concern for people in contemporary society? Which seems closest to the teachings of the Bible?

7. Study the concepts of "righteousness" and "justice" as used in the Bible. Are they interchangeable terms? What other words are used for them in modern translations of the Bible? On the basis of specific examples and instructions in the Scriptures,

can you compose a "Bible definition" of each, using modern language?

8. Look up "antinomianism" or the "antinomian heresy" in an encyclopedia, church history, or theology book. Why is it considered to be a heresy? Is it present in the modern world? How is it related to the fundamentalist-modernist controversy? How can this heresy be avoided?

9. Think of a church congregation which gives no direct attention to its social responsibilities and another which gives them much attention. What merits does each possess that are absent in the other? What flaws are present in each? Is it possible to eliminate the faults and increase the virtues of each by a middle-of-the-road policy that is not overbalanced by either an overemphasis or an underemphasis upon social concerns?

10. Find a church in your community or nearby which has a committee or board entrusted with social responsibilities. What are its duties? How is it organized? To whom is it responsible? What problems does it face? What have been its successes and failures?

RECOMMENDED READING

Lutheran Church - Missouri Synod, *Faith That Works by Love.* St. Louis, Mo.: Concordia, 1960. A guide for congregational welfare committees prepared by the Synod's Department of Social Welfare.

Niebuhr, H. Richard, *Christ and Culture.* New York: Harper, 1951 (Torchbook ed., 1956). A survey of the types of relationships between the church and society that have emerged in Christian history.

Nixon, Justin Wroe, *Responsible Christianity.* New York: Harper, 1950. Challenges to the Christian faith and ways in which responsible Christians serve as the leaven of a free society.

Rasmussen, Albert T., *Christian Social Ethics: Exerting Christian Influence.* Englewood Cliffs, N. J.: Prentice-Hall, 1956. A study of what the Christian response ought to be toward the enormous pressures and intimidations of the world.

Stotts, Herbert E., and Deats, Paul, Jr., *Methodism and Society: Guidelines for Strategy*. New York: Abingdon, 1962. Vol. IV in a series; relates findings of the other studies to social science insights in developing principles for a realistic strategy of social education, leadership, and action in the Methodist Church.

Webb, Muriel S., *The Social Ministry of the Local Church*. New York: National Council of the Churches of Christ in the U.S.A., 1956. A brief study guide for the use of local churches and church groups.

Chapter 6

Church-Sponsored Welfare

*If a brother or sister be naked, and destitute of daily food,
And one of you say unto them, Depart in peace, be ye
warmed and filled; notwithstanding ye give them not those
things which are needful to the body; what doth it profit?*

Even so faith, if it hath not works, is dead, being alone
(Jas. 2:15-17).

*And let us not be weary in well doing: for in due season
we shall reap, if we faint not.*

*As we have therefore opportunity, let us do good unto
all men, especially unto them who are of the household of
faith* (Gal. 6:9-10).

HISTORICALLY, CHRISTIAN CHURCHES HAVE PRACTICED "SEVEN COR-
poral Works of Mercy." They have fed the hungry, given drink
to the thirsty, clothed the naked, sheltered the homeless, visited
the sick and prisoners, ransomed captives, and buried the dead
(Matt. 25:34-44). They were a major influence on modern
humanitarian services.

Churches still sponsor a large number and wide variety of
social welfare programs. Many denominations support community centers or settlement houses in large cities. Hospitals, health
clinics, nursing homes for chronically ill and convalescent patients,
counseling centers, adoption agencies, gospel missions, recreational centers, child welfare services, retirement homes, day-care
nurseries, orphanages, camping programs, maternity homes, sheltered workshops for handicapped persons, chaplaincy services in
hospitals and other institutions, temperance organizations, services

to migrants, and overseas relief are but a few of the kinds of social welfare programs which have been officially sponsored by churches. Many also are helping to meet the expanding need for halfway houses to assist in the rehabilitation of the mentally ill, alcoholics, ex-convicts, and other persons after they have received more intensive treatment for their problems. Similarly home-care services, volunteer visitors programs, personal and family counseling, and other needs are being met through denominational and interdenominational agencies.

Church-related welfare services are provided on at least four levels of activity. Basic to all of them is the work of the local congregation. This traditionally includes a benevolent fund, sporadic volunteer services, casual visiting programs, prayers for the ill, financial support to denominational welfare agencies, and occasionally direct sponsorship of a retirement home, day-care nursery, community center, or other agency. These services ideally are supplemented by an active and direct concern to express and live the gospel in the daily affairs of members.

A second level is that of district, state, or other regional denominational units. Here are found projects like children's homes, retirement homes, health services, hospitals, chaplaincy programs, home-care services, and counseling centers.

On the denominational and interdenominational level, many services of the above types are provided. In addition, guidelines for church action are established, materials for use in Christian education are published, and colleges, universities, and seminaries are operated which help train personnel to meet welfare needs.

Cutting across all of these organized church activities is a fourth level: the involvement of individual Christians as citizens of both an earthly society and a heavenly community. This is usually the chief channel of church cooperation with non-church welfare agencies and programs.

The Changing Welfare Scene

In the modern world welfare services are handled more and more formally. Earlier, in an agrarian society, the children in a family were the main source of "retirement benefits." They supported the aged who were no longer productive economically. Neighbors assisted the disabled and bereaved with their farm work. Under this arrangement, formal programs of workmen's compensation, pension funds, unemployment insurance, and social security were not needed.

When the factory system began and people left home to work, sometimes moving across a continent, older forms of social welfare had to be replaced. The sick and the unemployed no longer had farm produce and an immediately present family to fall back upon in emergencies. The child left dependent on others by the death, divorce, disability, or desertion of a parent no longer could be cared for by the other adults in the family circle. A man temporarily disabled by an accident could not be helped with his work by a few hours of neighborly labor. Even the people next door in the impersonal city were apt to be strangers. Social services in a money-based economy cannot take the same form as social services in an agrarian subsistence-farming community.

Today the house-building and barn-raising system of the past has been replaced by credit unions and savings and loan associations. These in turn are supported by federal insurance programs to protect the interests of both investors and borrowers. Family care of the ill has been replaced by various types of private health insurance, government welfare programs, specialized private agencies to deal with specific problems, and public hospitals for the treatment of mentally ill, tubercular, epileptic, mentally retarded, and alcoholic patients. Personal and family aid to the elderly is increasingly replaced by private pension plans and governmental old age assistance and social security programs. These make it financially possible for the aged to live economically independent of their families in their own homes. The volunteer fire brigade is replaced by a professionally staffed and trained fire department. Mutual aid to a family whose property has been destroyed by a fire or tornado is replaced by fire and storm insurance. The relatively casual use of a spring, brook, lake, or private well for household water is replaced by government water and sewer systems, since the congestion of modern life makes the more primitive supplies dangerous sources of disease.

The expansion of government services may be seen, therefore, as a response to the needs of a new kind of society. Social legislation is an arrangement for providing mutual aid. Through taxes we pay into a fund. When a person has needs of a kind that is specified by law, he draws from the fund. While I may never "cash in" on the benefits, I am covered by a form of "social insurance" in case the need arises. As is the case with private insurance, many people pay in more than they take out while others take out more than they pay in. Indeed, I will be delighted if I never need to collect disability insurance under the Old Age, Survivors, and Disability Insurance provisions of the Social Security Act, just as I gladly fail to collect payments from my expensive automobile insurance. Private insurance covers only limited types of people, but social insurance may include everybody in the population.

Government welfare programs have expanded because people today are too mobile, too dependent upon fluctuations of the business cycle, too remote from subsistence farming, and too much controlled by social and economic forces over which they as individuals have no control to have their needs met solely by personal diligence and the resources of their immediate families.

It is therefore a mistake to say that government welfare programs arose because Christians failed to do their work. As long as Christians comprise but a fraction of the total population, they will be unable to meet all of its modern welfare needs through their agencies.

Church resources plus family resources met human needs passingly well in pre-industrial rural society. They are inadequate today because the needs are so vast and because even church members are not sufficiently motivated to "overextend" themselves in voluntary giving.

For the good of all society, all people must cooperate in providing welfare services. Some are thus "forced" to give what seems to be "more than their share," but those who complain the loudest about this "injustice" typically fail to recognize the extent to which their own wealth, income, and general well-being depend upon other people. They also are prone to overlook the fact that they are but stewards of their earthly possessions. They are their brothers' keepers.

A strong case can be made for the proposition that government welfare programs have arisen *because* Christians were doing their work, not because they failed. The diffusion of Christian values of mercy and love undoubtedly has helped to make the majority of people in our democratic society favor government programs to promote human dignity, self-respect, and happiness. The drive to reduce or eliminate such programs is spearheaded by extremists who lack a thorough understanding of modern society or are the pawns of selfish men of wealth who would stoop to any "honorable" means to reduce their own taxes and thus increase their discretionary income (income that can be spent any way they wish). In a religiously pluralistic society, no conceivable type of church program could begin to cope effectively with all social problems by itself.

This is not to say that church-sponsored welfare is now superfluous. In the past, churches have stimulated welfare programs. They have identified unmet needs and established activities to meet those needs. Then, when the sense of need had diffused throughout society, they often turned over many of these welfare services to other private or public agencies, sometimes again initiating new services to meet a new set of needs. Prisoners aid societies, foundling agencies, orphanages, alms for the poor, asylums for invalids and the feeble-minded, services to ex-slaves, and many other forms of charity are among the programs pioneered by churches and church people but now largely superseded by "secular" public and private programs. As the general public accepts a growing responsibility for material and physical aid, churches are released from that obligation to focus upon the more directly spiritual or nonmaterial needs of men.

Principles for Church Welfare Programs

In order to maintain a wholesome program of welfare services, conscientious study and evaluation should be a continual process. Some considerations worthy of attention in planning church-related welfare programs follow.

1. *Serve the whole man.* His needs extend beyond the spiritual into the areas of physical, economic, psychological, ethical, and social needs. The church must make sure that *all* these needs are met. Spiritual needs rooted in man's rebellion against God are often at the heart of the problems to which welfare services minister, but a narrowly conceived ministry to the "soul" will not clothe the naked and feed the hungry. Church programs that ignore the physical, social, and economic needs of

welfare clients are just as misguided as the secular ones that ignore men's psychological and spiritual needs. "Spiritual counsel" should complement, not replace, other welfare services.

2. *Remember the worth of man.* All people, regardless of skin color, nationality, social class, and circumstances, are created in God's image. Each has an inherent dignity which shoud be respected by welfare programs. His right to choose (within the limits of the law and reasonable measures of his capacity to do so) should not be violated by inflexible regulations that deny him the opportunity of growth through making responsible decisions. Welfare aid in the form of cash rather than in the form of meal tickets and material gifts usually gives greater opportunity for such growth. Just as God is willing to let man make mistakes, we should be willing to let those whom we help make mistakes even though a few will abuse the system.

Even the most unpromising derelict, from the human perspective, can be redeemed by God's grace. As God forgives the vilest of sinners who call upon Him, we must be ready to forgive those who need to make a new start in life. The first step in their recovery often occurs when they catch the vision of their own worth as persons for whom Christ died.

This means, too, that whenever there is a clash between "property rights" and "human rights," Christians must give allegiance to the latter. A man's life does not consist of the abundance or lack of his possessions (Luke 12:15).

3. *Relate welfare services to the total task of the church.* As we have seen, church-sponsored welfare is related to evangelistic and educational goals. It has a place in the local church, on the associational or regional level, in the denomination, in the total work of churches as cooperating units, and in their relationships to society. Nothing should be done on the national level which can be accomplished more effectively on the state or regional level, and nothing should be done regionally which can be done more effectively on the local church level. All areas of Christian social welfare should supplement each other; they should not compete as if they were totally unrelated programs.

4. *Distinguish "felt needs" from factual needs.* The experiences of one or a few individuals do not by themselves provide a reliable indicator of services which churches ought to provide.

The "faith missions" tradition has encouraged the development of numerous necessary services, but it has also made it easy for charlatans, impostors, and swindlers to form honorable-sounding organizations and solicit funds without ever providing the services they publicize.

As in other Christian service, the "call" which is experienced only by its recipient may indicate personal psychological problems rather than represent the work of the Holy Spirit. If God calls, the call will be evident to other Christians. A church should gather reliable evidence about an alleged need through community surveys, interviews with leaders of relevant institutions, community welfare councils, and other research.

5. *Make welfare primarily a lay ministry.* The clergyman has only a limited number of hours each week. He cannot do everything, as he must concentrate on the duties for which he is professionally trained. Much of the Christian pastor's visiting, his professional counseling, and even his pulpit ministry have direct and indirect welfare implications. He ought to uphold welfare as a part of his total ministry, but the details of administering and coordinating church welfare services and activities should be entrusted to capable laymen, as was done in the apostolic church (Acts 6:1-7). In many instances these laymen will be professional people meeting welfare needs as part of their daily work (Chapter 8), but in others they will be chiefly volunteers coordinated by professional people in various agencies (Chapter 9). Some congregations may employ social workers, clinical psychologists, or other professional persons to help meet these needs. The burden must not be cast on the shoulders of an already overloaded professional ministry.

6. *Maintain a wholesome balance between institutional provisions and individual services.* In order to minister to the "whole man," due attention must be given to social and psychological needs as well as to economic services and a spiritual ministry. Hence routine services should be supplemented by personal kindnesses which professional people seldom have time to give. To assume that all needs are met by rote services is as fallacious as assuming that helping a few individuals relieves one of responsibility to correct social, economic, or political maladjustments which lead to their misery. Christian compassion must extend in

practice as well as in theory to both "the multitudes" and individual persons.

7. *Extend Christian compassion beyond the social boundaries of the church.* As we have seen, loving as God loves means loving the whole world, not only those in a cozy Christian fellowship who will amply return one's love (Luke 6:32-36). Providing the services of a church-related agency to those who are not members of its congregations is one way to proclaim the Christian message to the world.

8. *Cooperate with community welfare agencies.* Christians should cooperate with public and private agencies which meet human needs. These needs go far beyond the time, personnel, funds, and other resources of the church as an institution. Cooperation is an absolute necessity for meeting the needs of unwed mothers, senile citizens, alcoholics, disabled workers, retarded children, the mentally ill, the divorced, juvenile delinquents, criminals, and others who have special needs.

No compromise of basic Christian doctrine is involved in cooperation with typical welfare agencies. Most have a highly qualified staff which is dedicated to helping people. By lending moral and spiritual support as well as financial assistance, Christian citizens will gain the respect of their neighbors and will be represented in the decision-making process through board memberships and committee activities. If, on the contrary, their involvement is limited to negative criticism on occasions when they fear that some Christian principle is violated, they will lose both the respect of many fellow citizens and the privilege of helping to shape new decisions. Through a process of "Christian infiltration" as well as through personal friendships with leaders, organizational memberships, committee work, political participation, and cooperation in significant welfare projects, Christians can influence the chief decision makers of the community.

Participation in community councils and other cooperative agencies which plan community services demonstrates the concern of the church and its people for man's social needs. It helps to prevent the total secularization of welfare programs in American society. It is a source of mutual encouragement to church-related programs and projects and gives ideas for more effective service. It helps to prevent a wasteful duplication of costly services by several agencies aiming to meet the same needs. It informs Christians about resources to which needy cases can be referred when specialized help is advisable. It involves collaboration with "the world" only in specific areas of activity for which Christians are commanded to have concern. Usually there is no choice; either one cooperates with existing agencies or the services to human needs will not be furnished at all in the local community.

The church should strengthen and approve the good that is present in society, doing its utmost to see that each needy person is guaranteed the proper amount of help and often going the "second mile" in giving assistance beyond that which other agencies can provide.

When social services for particular needs are met adequately through existing agencies, church-related projects should seek out needs that are not being met rather than step into a competitive program which entices clients, staff, or finances away from other agencies. The needs of the world are so great that it is far better to fill unmet needs than to duplicate existing programs, even if they are not strictly "Christian." Duplication represents unwise stewardship.

9. *Distinguish welfare from evangelism.* The assumption that the primary end of welfare ministries is "soul-winning" may lead to a failure either to win souls or to provide effective services to people in need. Giving a cup of water in Christ's name will bring its reward even if it never results directly in conversions (Mark 9:41).

God has given different tasks to the members of the Christian church (I Cor. 12). Administrators of church welfare programs have the primary duty of providing welfare services. If they make evangelism their primary goal, the welfare program is apt to suffer, to the ultimate detriment of the evangelistic effort itself. Many victims of social problems are not very capable of making the most important decision of life while they are ill. When they have been healed, they will be better subjects for direct evangelism. Words without deeds of love are not likely to bear the fruit of conversion. Meanwhile, everything that God's people do in His name has an evangelistic dimension, so even "purely welfare work" helps to promote the evangelistic cause. If the church is present through its members or services at the place and hour of human need, it will find many "teachable moments" during which people will receive the gospel.

The mixing of primary goals can cause confusion, misunderstanding, and a failure to achieve *any* of the objectives. When professional ministers are freed from social welfare activities to concentrate attention upon nonmaterial needs, they will do a better job of evangelism and education. When church social workers are freed from a specifically evangelistic responsibility that counts success in terms of conversions, they will do a better job of social work.

10. *Maintain high standards of service.* The process of giving help involves far more than personal piety and good intentions by the helper. Some Christians oppose high professional standards in church welfare programs in the name of "stewardship" to save a few dollars. When their voice is heeded, the world receives the impression that anything the church gives in the name of Christ must be shoddy and cheap. Assigning agency supervision to novices who are castoffs of other professions implies that those served by the agency are unimportant.

Church agencies should set the pace in meeting welfare needs. They should maintain the very highest of professional standards. Professional qualifications of training and experience protect the integrity of the agency, the financial investments of contributors, and especially the dignity and well-being of clients.

11. *Seek the best, not merely the good.* Numerous ventures in foreign and home missions, education, welfare, and social recreational programs are possible in the typical church. All of these may be good in and of themselves. Specialized institutions could be established by churches to meet a wide variety of human needs. Homes for retarded children, adoption services, nursing homes, halfway houses for the mentally ill, counseling clinics, alcoholic rehabilitation centers, and a wide variety of other agencies could be established by churches. But such facilities and programs are very costly in terms of personnel, facilities, and finances. They would divert time, money, leadership, and other resources from existing church programs. They thus might weaken or eliminate other, perhaps more effective, forms of Christian witness. Evaluative research is hence of great importance in the work of Jesus Christ. What He wants men to do

is often clarified by a study of the costs and other consequences of each of several alternatives of action. Christians should seek to do "their utmost for His highest," never content with second-best when the best is attainable. They must remember that the good may be the enemy of the best.

12. *Retain flexibility.* Although people remain basically the same, their environment and the state of technology do not. Valid programs of one generation may be a hindrance to Christ's cause in the next. The traditional orphanage, for example, has been outmoded by recent social developments. Retirement homes may be abandoned in the future and replaced by new forms of independent housing, family care services, and foster homes. Mental hospitals may be succeeded by noninstitutional forms of treatment.

New needs require new patterns of action, and new social developments may make old patterns obsolete. To sanctify traditional organizations and programs as if they are eternally and unchangeably valid is a form of idolatry (see Matt. 15:1-9; Mark 7:1-13; Col. 2:8).

Precautions for Church Welfare

Many dangers must be avoided if church welfare programs are to achieve their objectives. Preceding discussions have clarified most of them enough so that they need no more than brief mention.

1. *Don't try to be neutral.* Social problems confront men daily in the modern world. Churches and Christians who ignore them in effect say that they have no compassion for the unfortunate victims, that they lack the constraining love of Christ, or that the gospel has no relevance to problems of human need. Failure to act on social welfare needs is like failure to vote in many elections; no vote is a "No" vote. Neutrality on community welfare programs is impossible.

2. *Don't shun all ecumenical programs.* If churches are to sponsor welfare programs, they often must cooperate across denominational lines in order to have the necessary strength of finances and constituency. Some evangelicals have assumed that cooperation with denominations which have different doctrinal interpretations involves a compromise of the gospel. Their

position is, however, not consistent. They cooperate in military and institutional chaplaincy programs without doctrinal compromise. They are glad when any group works with them to combat the liquor traffic. They work with Unitarians and Jews to combat the use of tax funds for Catholic parochial schools.

Doing good is a virtue in its own right, so cooperation with others in specific projects to do good is completely acceptable. Such arrangements are different from mergers and other programs which cut across all areas of activity. They are not the same as cooperation along specifically religious lines, which might involve a compromise of basic doctrines.

All American religions share a basic concern for justice, good will in community relations, humanitarian social services, integrity and honesty in government, crime prevention, rehabilitation of delinquents, and opposition to the materialistic philosophies of secularism and Communism. They can work with each other in social welfare and social action programs to promote those values in society. Such cooperation is good stewardship, for it reduces the duplication of costly services, extends Christian love to many areas of human need, and makes it easier to locate services available to clients of particular kinds.

Billy Graham's words on cooperation are instructive:

> Nowhere in the Bible does it teach that we are to withdraw ourselves from society. Rather, it teaches quite the contrary. We are to join with others who are working to good purpose to help lift the unfortunate.[1]

Graham indicates that it is fear that makes one unwilling to listen to another viewpoint — the petty fear that one's own ideas "may not be unassailable." Jesus lacked such fear, for He knew the difference between graciousness and compromise. He had

> the most open and all-encompassing mind that this world has ever seen. His own inner conviction was so strong, so firm, so unswerving that He could afford to mingle with any group secure in the knowledge that He would not be contaminated.[2]

Followers of Christ will not let misinterpretations of the ecumenical movement prevent them from doing good.

[1] *Peace with God* (Garden City, N. Y.: Doubleday, 1953), p. 198.
[2] *Ibid.*, p. 202.

3. *Don't imply that man lives by bread alone.* It is easy for Christian welfare programs to slip into the false assumption that their responsibilities have been fulfilled when material needs are met. People want to be loved, to have meaningful roles through which they can contribute to society, to feel wanted, to be independent enough to make their own decisions, and to have the self-respect which is fostered by the respect of others for them. Overattention to the body and its needs can disguise or deny the fact that Christians have hope beyond the grave. A wholesome combination of spiritual ministries with physical, economic, psychological, and social services ought to characterize church-related welfare programs.

4. *Don't be blind to needs.* It is easy for Christians to get into a rut of daily activity that makes them blind to the misery of others. Middle-class suburban dwellers are not apt to realize that many people in their own metropolitan area live in poverty. Churches which move from the inner city to the suburbs often leave behind and forget elderly, disabled, mentally deficient, and other economically and socially marginal members. Because they are out of sight, they become out of mind. Christians should not overlook their ministry to "the least" of Christ's brethren.

5. *Don't stereotype.* The tendency to assume that all members of a social category like Negroes, juvenile delinquents, alcoholics, divorcees, or the elderly are alike must be avoided. Every person is distinct from all others in his capacities, interests, personality, opportunities, problems, needs, and responsibilities. Social services must allow for these individual differences. No one pat solution automatically meets the needs of all members of a social category.

6. *Don't let ulterior motives control the program.* Christian welfare work is sometimes burdened by egocentric workers who use condescending pity and self-indulgent patronage in order to prove their own superiority. They frequently insist on direct forms of personal giving to the unfortunate so that they will receive the immediate rewards of gratitude from the recipients. This kind of motivation, and the type of program resulting from it, must be avoided strenuously. Emphasizing ministries to individual persons at the expense of social action programs directed toward large-scale reforms can actually give an indirect blessing to evils which flow from selfishness, covetousness, and the love

115

of money. These are forms of mammon-worship or idolatry (Matt. 6:24; Luke 16:10-15; Eph. 5:5; Col. 3:5; I Tim. 6:6-10; Heb. 13:5; etc.). Even those who argue that church welfare must be provided in order to keep taxes down may be guilty of an unchristian aloofness from public action to correct the larger dimensions of human suffering.

7. *Don't become a victim of institutionalism.* Making the church or its agencies a false god to be served rather than a servant is another form of idolatry. "Supporting the church" is not necessarily the same as "supporting the Kingdom of God." The goal of church ministries should not be to strengthen the organization for its own sake. The church as an institution should promote human welfare, not stand in its way. The maintenance tasks necessary to perpetuate an institution's activities should never become its primary goals.

Sponsoring social welfare activities just to keep up with the "ecclesiastical Joneses" also may lead a church in unwholesome directions. Every church is different. Each, hence, should have a somewhat different set of activities, looking to God for direction, not to neighboring congregations.

8. *Don't wait for all motives to be pure.* If we wait for complete selflessness in social action programs, we will never act. The rewards of reciprocity are present in all social services. Helping others is an indirect form of social insurance that helps to protect us in case of our own future need. There is a degree of self-interest in everything that men do. Since we are told to love our neighbors as we love ourselves (Lev. 19:18; Matt. 19:19; 22:39; Rom. 13:9; Gal. 5:14; etc.), this is not inconsistent with Christian ethics.

9. *Don't let the dollar sign separate you from God's will.* Social services are costly, so the cost should be reckoned in planning them. But cost by itself should not be the primary consideration in attempting to determine God's will.

An emphasis upon tithing may lead economically prosperous Christians to feel that their financial obligations to God are fulfilled by giving one-tenth of their income to the church. Fund-raising may also give the impression that the church's concern is only with its own treasury, that monetary gifts purchase spiritual merit, or that the church is an organization to be served rather than an instrument of service. Materialistic considerations can thus distort men's conceptions of Christian service and interfere with achieving God's will.

10. *Don't usurp professional help.* Volunteer visitors at the bedside of physically sick persons perform significant services that promote physical and spiritual health, but they cannot take the place of the medical doctor. The same is true in regard to the services of social workers, psychiatrists, clinical psychologists, lawyers, and public health nurses. Good intentions, piety, and Christian motivations are supplements of, not substitutes for, professional knowledge and skills.

11. *Don't condemn the sinner.* Moral condemnation of sin should not be confused with condemnation of the person who sins. He remains a person created in the image of God, one for whom Christ died.

All have sinned. Some sins are more obvious than others, but this is not an acceptable basis for a legalistic self-righteousness that stands in the way of accepting the person who sinned. Censure and condemnation alienate. Loving trust and confidence win and reform sinners. Just as God accepts and loves the sinner without excusing the sin, the children of God should extend their love, help, and expectation or hope of redemption. Demonstrating Christian acceptance is a major need in both welfare and evangelism. God loves men as they are. Love imparts the hope of personal renewal to its recipients. Just as God became flesh and dwelt among men in order to communicate with man on his own level, Christians must go to people on their own level in order to reach them.

Supporting social services for divorcees, ex-convicts, juvenile delinquents, the children of unwed mothers, alcoholics, homosexuals, and prostitutes is not the equivalent of supporting vice, blessing immorality, praising crime, or sanctifying sin. Neither is moral condemnation of these evils by itself an effective means of preventing and treating them. Morality cannot be forced on people. It results from an inner response to love when there is freedom to make decisions. To make aid depend upon the "morality" of recipients is to force "Christian morals" on non-

117

christians or to insist upon change before the help that makes change possible has been given.

12. *Don't act without planning.* Count all foreseeable costs before beginning new social services lest they later must be disgracefully dropped (see Luke 14:25-33). Social needs seem to be without limit. Research is necessary to determine how much and which welfare services a church or denomination ought to provide.

Problems of securing competent professional leadership, moral and spiritual support, and adequate finances have made many church-related welfare programs very insecure and weak. A Protestant denomination of even as many as a million members scattered over the nation cannot expect to have the same size and scope of welfare services as those under Roman Catholic or Jewish auspices. No simple rule of thumb indicates how large a constituency must be to establish a successful adoption agency, child welfare program, institution for the mentally retarded, or other welfare project. Careful research is necessary for an adequate consideration of each proposal.

Effects of Church Welfare Programs

If they are competently administered, church welfare services will relieve suffering and promote the well-being of people who are in need. They will indirectly stimulate evangelism.

Church welfare will influence Christians who support the work with their giving, prayers, and volunteer services. They will become more aware of the many-faced types of human need. Their sympathy toward and understanding of people from all levels of life who have problems will increase. They will grow in spiritual grace and Christlikeness.

Many congregations have been revitalized by giving attention to the social welfare needs of people in the surrounding community. For instance, St. Andrew's Memorial Church in Detroit, an Episcopal congregation, was losing strength. Even a neighborhood canvass of the parish brought no results, for people saw no reason for paying any attention to a church that never paid attention to them. But then the church became concerned for the living needs of families. It employed part-time university students to bring children to the church and furnished cooperative activities for them, some of these activities having a directly religious content. As a result, the church reversed its gradual decline in membership and again began to grow.[3] Other examples of similar renewal with a social service outreach are the Douglas Park Covenant Church in Chicago under the leadership of the Rev. John Wiens, and Elim Baptist Church in Minneapolis.[4]

It is true of churches as well as of individual Christians that losing one's life in service is the way to abundant life. People whose social, physical, and material needs are met by church welfare services are more likely to respond to the church's gospel than those whose "non-spiritual" needs are ignored by the church.

The results of Christian social service are in God's hands. There may be no tangible earthly returns. The greatest reward of all will be the Lord's "Well done!" when His Kingdom is fully established (Matt. 25:14-40).

SUGGESTIONS FOR DISCUSSION AND STUDY

1. What welfare services or agencies are supported by the missionary and benevolent funds of your church? Why are they helped? Do they represent wise stewardship?

2. What welfare services does your denomination support (1) on foreign mission fields, (2) in home missions, and (3) in your metropolitan area or geographic region? Is there a difference between its perspective toward welfare projects at home and abroad? Why? Is it sponsoring more or fewer welfare services now than in the past? Can you explain this change?

3. Once a church has established a welfare program, should it ever withdraw from it by transferring it to another agency, by changing the services it offers, or by discontinuing it? Why or why not?

[3] G. Paul Musselman, *The Church on the Urban Frontier* (Greenwich, Conn.: Seabury Press, 1960) , pp. 70-71.

[4] See the description of the latter by its pastor, the Rev. Emmett V. Johnson, "The Ministry: Challenge in the Changing Inner City," *Bethel Seminary Quarterly*, XII (May, 1964) , 61-69.

4. What should be the chief purpose or goal of church-sponsored welfare services? Are there other secondary goals? Is it ethical to emphasize one set of goals in fund-raising campaigns and another in the daily work of the program?

5. How do the welfare activities of your church compare with those of other local congregations? What arguments are given by the ministers and lay leaders of the churches for church action or inaction in the area of welfare?

6. What welfare projects of other groups can you conscientiously support without any compromise of your faith? What are the objections of some Christians to cooperating with certain specific ecumenical or non-church agencies which are represented in your community? Check to discover which of these objections are the result of facts and which are based upon ungrounded opinions of prejudiced persons.

7. Visit one or more church-sponsored social agencies. Learn about more than its physical facilities. Whom does it serve? How are they introduced to its program? What are the qualifications and duties of the staff? What standards of service does it maintain? Does it have well-defined objectives toward which it works consistently? What are the sources of its financial support? What problems does it face? Can you or your church help to meet its needs?

8. Visit a public or private social agency that is not church-related. Get the same kinds of information as in Question 7, but also learn about its relationships to churches and clergymen. How does it differ from church-sponsored agencies which provide similar services?

9. Discuss the changes that have occurred in welfare services to elderly people in your community. How does their own status today compare with that of their grandparents two generations ago? What happened during their childhood to people who had welfare needs of various kinds (unemployment, disablement by accident, orphans, widows, feeble-minded children, mental illness or "lunacy," illegitimacy, juvenile delinquency, imprisonment, poverty, alcoholism, and the like)? How does that compare with the present situation? Are differences be-

tween the past and present brought about by changes in people or by changes in their social environment?

10. Identify the most acute unmet needs for social services in your community. (Interviews with judges, probation and parole officers, police, social workers, medical doctors, hospital administrators, public health officials, family counselors, bank credit advisors, lawyers, schoolteachers and administrators, city planners, and employment counselors will help.) How can these needs be met? Should your church take an active part in satisfying them or in stimulating others to provide them?

RECOMMENDED READING

Feucht, Oscar E. editor, *Helping Families through the Church*. St. Louis, Mo.: Concordia, 1957. A symposium on family-life education which indicates how the church can serve the needs of families.

Grant, Fern Babcock, *Ministries of Mercy*. New York: Friendship Press, 1962. Church-sponsored services for children and youth, the aging, the physically and mentally ill, the handicapped, unmarried mothers, alcoholics, drug addicts, the economically dependent, migrants, prisoners, parolees, and ex-convicts.

Gray, Robert M., and Moberg, David O., *The Church and the Older Person*. Grand Rapids, Mich.: Eerdmans, 1962. A survey of studies relating religion to adjustment in old age and a summary of suggestions on what the church can do for older people and what they can do for the church.

Harrington, Janette T., and Webb, Muriel S., *Who Cares?* New York: Friendship Press, 1962. A project guidebook on the church's mission to persons of special need.

Keith-Lucas, Alan, *The Church and Social Welfare*. Philadelphia: Westminster Press, 1962. A brief analysis and critique of the welfare picture in America today and of Protestant theology in relationship to it. "Required reading" for every Christian who is in welfare work and for all who are concerned in any way with relationships between welfare and Christianity.

Miller, Haskell M., *Compassion and Community*. New York: Association Press, 1961. A survey and appraisal of the church's changing role in social welfare.

Palmer, Charles E., *The Church and the Exceptional Person*. New York: Abingdon Press, 1961. How to locate and serve persons with impaired hearing or vision, those who are intellectually gifted or retarded, and the crippled, speech handicapped, emotionally disturbed, institutionalized, home-bound, and multi-handicapped.

Chapter 7

The Church and the "Secular World"

Our Father which art in heaven, . . . Thy will be done in
earth, as it is in heaven (Matt. 6:9-10).

Ye are the salt of the earth: but if the salt have lost his
savour, wherewith shall it be salted? it is thenceforth good
for nothing, but to be cast out, and to be trodden under foot
of men.

Ye are the light of the world. A city that is set on an hill
cannot be hid.

Neither do men light a candle, and put it under a bushel,
but on a candlestick; and it giveth light unto all that are
in the house.

Let your light so shine before men, that they may see your
good works, and glorify your Father which is in heaven
(Matt. 5:13-16).

THE WELFARE SERVICES OF THE CHURCH MUST BE COORDINATED
with those of other agencies at many points. Most specialized
needs of people cannot be furnished directly by church-related
programs. Moreover, even in those churches which support
extensive social service projects, individuals who are suddenly
engulfed in social problems may be unaware of the available
help. Hence it is desirable for every congregation to have a
social welfare committee or a liaison person who will provide the
necessary guidance for its needy members. As society becomes
more complex and as population increases, this type of service
will become increasingly important and essential.

The church and community agencies can cooperate in studying

welfare needs and planning future services. Men of good will are much more numerous than certain members of separatistic religious groups would expect. Christian values pertinent to social needs are widely diffused throughout society. Numerous nonchristians share them and are glad to help implement them within the limits of their time and other resources. Some people outside the church are even more concerned for such needs than the average church member. They feel that Christians are hypocrites because of their lack of social concern. Demonstrating Christian love helps to promote evangelism among such persons.

The church also cooperates with welfare agencies through its members' vocations and the volunteer services they provide. (See Chapters 8 and 9.) Our chief focus in this chapter will be upon social action. This inevitably overlaps with social welfare programs, which often are established by such action.

Secular social services can teach the church many lessons, just as the church can teach them. Alcoholics Anonymous, for example, can teach Christians how to discover people with special problems and how to evangelize them in a ministry of compassionate fellowship. It recognizes that people are part of a society which puts many unavoidable pressures upon them. It demonstrates the therapeutic power of fellowship groups. Other agencies and programs have equally significant lessons for Christian service.

Church Resolutions

A common practice among religious denominations in democratic societies is the writing and passing of resolutions dealing with contemporary political, economic, and social conditions. These may be given publicity through press releases. They are printed in the denomination's annual reports. Copies are sometimes sent to influential persons in politics and other areas of life. Occasionally sermons are based upon them, and adult education classes may study them. Most often, however, they are buried in historical archives and never brought to the attention of lay members of local churches. A Chicago research study revealed, for example, that only one-tenth of the chairmen of church boards of trustees had any personal acquaintance with major resolutions passed in their denominational assembly. Fewer than three out of every hundred knew of any effort to inform the congregation about them.[1]

Resolutions may give outsiders an impression of unity in a religious group even when they are passed by a bare majority of delegates who are not representative of the denominational membership. Whenever a church acts like a pressure group speaking on behalf of all its members, it runs the risk of becoming "committed" to a position or to methods of lobbying and other action of which a majority of its members may not approve. Obviously, a church "divided against itself" because of these complexities will have diminished social effectiveness in its community.

Resolutions can be criticized on other grounds besides their apparent ineffectiveness. Sometimes they serve merely to appease the conscience; they substitute for more direct action that "gets hands dirty" in problems like local option, open occupancy, or civil rights.

Pronouncements by church councils at times seem to represent a summary of human wisdom that replaces the guidance of the Scriptures. The expression of sweeping platitudes inapplicable to modern realities may assist the forces of evil as much as the forces of good, for they encourage people to ignore religious principles entirely. Church spokesmen also are prone to confuse some contemporary "Caesar's" cause with the cause of God. Having first reached a conclusion on the basis of their "secular" social class or occupational involvements, they then seek a scriptural "foundation" or rationalization for it.

We must ever be on guard against abuse of the Bible. The devil quotes Scripture for his own purposes (Matt. 4:6; cf. II Cor. 11:14-15; Jas. 2:19). Resolutions should be based on sound theology and hermeneutics (principles of Bible interpretation). The Bible should take precedence over secular authority, not vice versa. But at the same time Christian principles must be applied to the realities of the contemporary world revealed by the social sciences. Prayer, Bible study, and a sincere desire to

---

[1] Victor Obenhaus, "Protestant Social Policy: Why Isn't It More Effective?" *The Nation*, CLXXVII (Aug. 1, 1953), 91-93. See also David O. Moberg, *The Church as a Social Institution* (Englewood Cliffs, N. J.: Prentice-Hall, 1962), pp. 147-149, 385.

be led by the Holy Spirit also will help to formulate truly Christian resolutions.

Resolutions do perform important functions in the Christian church and modern society in spite of all their limitations. Their greatest benefit probably falls upon those who are involved in studying the issues, formulating resolutions about them, and pounding out the final statements in small groups with the hammer of discussion.

Resolutions remind church people that their Christian obligations extend far beyond the walls of the church building. They help to show the world that Christianity is relevant to the conditions and problems of modern life. They help ministers and laymen articulate their convictions. They give pastors and teachers moral support for the proclamation of Christian truth on controversial issues on which they lack the full support of their congregations. Their educational impact and social control effects make them play an important role among church people even when they are ignored by the rest of society. Resolutions are a legitimate and important part of the "prophetic voice" of the Christian church.

The Church and Government

Government is the system of authoritative direction, control, rule, and restraint over the actions of men within a geographic area. Because we tend to think of government in terms of a territory, we sometimes fail to recognize that any governmental unit consists ultimately of people, those who are ruled as well as the rulers. The tendency to personalize governments in terms of their leaders makes us forget that these leaders are symbolic representatives, not the nation itself.

A government is basically an agency of the people. It is established to serve them. Even the most authoritarian government is ultimately subject in some degree to the will of the people over whom it rules. If a governmental agency or institution ever becomes in effect an object of worship, with men existing only to promote the state, Christian values have been perverted and a form of idolatry established. Christian concern for the whole man leads to a concern for government on the local, state, national, and international levels.

Although the Christian church is not a political institution, it must be concerned with many basic issues and trends in political institutions. Churches speak through resolutions on issues which have religious and moral implications. (Are there any issues which do not?) They influence members to vote, and sometimes to vote in a specific way, on particular issues and candidates. They stimulate youth to consider entering political vocations. They lobby on such issues as liquor control, civil liberties, control of vice, and church-state relations. They educate citizens on subjects related to their political responsibilities. They give their members experience in church government and thus train them in the skills of political discussion and action.

Churches should give political leaders and government administrators credit for wise action and moral conduct. They should not communicate with them only when something seems so wrong that condemnation appears to be in order. Reminding them of desirable legislation helps to promote what is good; when churches speak only to criticize, they give the impression that Christianity is purely negativistic.

Because political issues are so complex, church members seldom face clear black and white choices and hence are often divided into opposing camps. Each political party represents a variety of positions and interests, some of which may be unquestionably consistent with Christian values and others highly doubtful. Some candidates may be fine Christians, while others in the same party may be immoral or dishonest. Proposed legislation may represent an admixture of Christian and unchristian values. For such reasons, it is unwise for a church to become linked with any one political party. It should work actively for that which is merciful and just in the platforms and programs of all parties, and it should oppose injustice, mercilessness, and the lack of love in all.

As individual citizens, however, church members should be active in the political parties of their choice. Devout Christians are found in both major American political parties. The church ought to support them with prayer and other sanctions. People who are willing to be active in their party on the local precinct level will be put to work quickly in an election year. Such workers are absolutely essential to our entire democratic political structure.

The Christian who works diligently in a political party on

the local level will be heard there when he speaks. His faithfulness will soon lead to influence on the district and state levels where many basic decisions of the political parties are made.

Since the law educates people and helps to form their character, it is a very important channel for the exercise of Christian influence. It is true that what is inside man cannot be changed directly by legislation, but law does control outward conduct. Laws establish and maintain order in society. They protect people against immoral conduct like murder and theft. Civil rights laws on such matters as equal opportunities for all people gradually remove the inequalities of education and occupational status that perpetuate false images or stereotypes of minority groups. They thus help to promote conduct which upholds human dignity and morality.

Social Legislation

The term "social legislation" applies to laws which are designed to improve and protect the economic and social position of groups of people. It is aimed primarily at improving the condition of those who are unable to achieve healthful or decent living standards for themselves because of limitations of age, sex, race, physical disability, mental defects, education, or economic problems. It also applies to programs aimed at preventing similar deprivation among persons who currently live on an adequate level. It includes laws which protect working women, prevent abuses of child labor, help the unemployed, meet the needs of dependent children, control the distribution and treat the effects of alcohol and narcotic drugs, aid the needy blind, furnish workmen's compensation for on-the-job accidents, establish social insurance programs for retirement, disability, and death, rehabilitate socially inadequate people, provide treatment for tuberculosis, mental illness, and mental retardation, and meet a wide variety of similar needs of people who live in mass society.

There are such strong feelings about these modern developments that many people respond to them emotionally in terms of propaganda slogans like "creeping socialism" and "the welfare state." Their feelings interfere with adequate interpretation and prevent them from acting rationally when they are confronted with citizenship responsibilities related to social legislation. Christians need to understand social legislation and appraise it realistically.

We already noted (Chapter 4) that social legislation in the United States goes back to the very founding of the nation. It is not a product of the century in which socialism emerged as a prominent political and economic philosophy. The Government of the United States was founded to "promote the general welfare" (among other objectives). Our increasingly industrialized and urban society, in which all men are closely interdependent, demands an expansion of social services by government; privately sponsored alternatives inevitably fail to meet the needs of a substantial minority, if not the majority, of the population. The welfare of all is linked with the welfare of all others; to promote the general welfare, government must promote the welfare of all segments of the population.

Most opponents to social legislation are inconsistent. They typically desire special protection, subsidies, or other benefits for their own occupational or economic group (business, farming, labor, etc.), yet violently oppose equivalent forms of help to others. When they themselves are helped by government, they believe that "free enterprise" is boosted and everybody is helped as a result. They do not realize that the same arguments can be used on behalf of much legislation they oppose, because their vision is distorted by the "colored glasses" of stereotypes. They forget that, because of man's sinful self-seeking, the "perfect love" of completely voluntary giving by those who have this world's goods to those who do not (I Tim. 6:18) cannot be depended upon to meet the full impact of suffering from social problems in our complex world.

Christians must take special precautions against such biases. They should strive to form as accurate a picture of society as it is possible for finite human beings to have.

Most social legislation can be interpreted as "love in action." The desire to protect one's own future is undoubtedly interwoven with concern for the needs of others in the passage of such laws, but this is an aspect of loving others as one loves himself. The shortcomings of men make it all the more urgent that laws enforce an institutionalized form of compassion, for without such legislation the weak would suffer even more than they do. There will still be ample room for personal demonstrations of voluntary assistance, since numerous needs cannot be fully satisfied through legislative action. Christian compassion is evident in cheerfully paying taxes to help meet welfare needs as well as in voluntary contributions to charities and gifts to specific persons in need.

Two forms of social legislation are often confused with each other. *Public assistance* in the U. S. includes Old Age Assistance, Aid to the Families of Dependent Children, Aid to the Blind, Aid to the Permanently and Totally Disabled, and Medical Assistance to the Aged. All of these are subsidized by federal funds. In addition, General Assistance is distributed solely by local and state governments. Every public assistance program is financed entirely by taxation and does not depend upon prior contributions by the recipients. *Social insurance,* on the other hand, is financed jointly by employers and employees. Payments are based on wages or salaries received by the worker. The Social Security program includes both public assistance and social insurance.

Public assistance is typically accompanied by a *means test* to determine the nature and extent of need. The test determines whether assistance is to be granted and the amount to be received by the needy person. Means tests are necessary in our type of society to avoid abuses, but at times they become a source of injustice. They usually provide for a level of living below that of the poorest workingmen in the community. They are often behind the times in an era of rising costs of living, for they are set by law or administrative action at a level of, for example, the cost of living in 1955 or 1960 when prices were lower than at present. They often require the recipient to use up all of his wealth and property. The state often takes a lien on any remaining property and has first priority in settling estates. To receive help, one must truly be a pauper. The accompanying social stigma and damage to self-images may in turn lead to additional social and psychological problems.

The beneficiaries of public assistance, in other words, must prove that they are indigent. The standards used and the administration of these programs depend upon state laws, so they vary widely, even though most of them are supported by federal as well as by state and local tax funds.

Social Insurance

The two most important social insurance programs in the United States are Old Age and Survivor's Disability Insurance (OASDI) and Unemployment Insurance. Both are provisions of the Social Security Act. OASDI is an income maintenance program for retired or disabled workers and a source of economic support for the dependent survivors of workers. It covers about nine-tenths of all gainfully employed workers.

"Social security," as it is commonly called, is a contributory system. Citizens pay for the benefits they later receive. Retirement benefits are based upon previous earnings and do not depend upon any test of means or need. There are no limits upon bank savings, investments, and real property which the person receiving retirement benefits may possess, but limits are placed upon the amount of money retired workers may earn by employment while receiving them. During the productive working life of the employer the government currently collects 3 5/8 percent of the employee's earnings up to $4800 per year and another 3 5/8 percent from his employer (5 4/10 percent from self-employed persons) under the Federal Insurance Contribution Act for this program.

OASDI is not solely a "pension plan," for it also indicates protection against disability and insurance provisions in the event of death of a worker. People who compare the cost of a private pension plan with OASDI to "prove" that it would be cheaper to finance their own program typically forget to include the added costs of these other insurance provisions.

Unemployment insurance helps workers whose income is temporarily interrupted by work stoppages and layoffs. In most states unemployment compensation is paid for a maximum of twenty-six weeks, so it does not meet the full needs of major economic depressions. Like OASDI it is a contributory program. It is financed by a tax upon employers based upon wages paid, but employees pay indirectly by receiving relatively lower wages than they otherwise might and by paying somewhat higher prices for consumer products. Only those who have been covered by "wage credits" and are available for work and seek work are eligible for the benefits.

The insurance principle of spreading insurable risks is the

131

foundation of social insurance. It is *social* in the sense that individual policies are not made out and large numbers are covered on a group basis. As social insurance has expanded, public assistance payments have proportionately decreased in the corresponding categories.

Commercial insurance companies, the American Medical Association, and other influential groups with vested interests have persistently attacked social insurance. They have claimed that it is not genuine insurance, that it is not an effective form of savings, and that it is too costly.

It is true that social insurance is not an annuity contract like many types of life insurance. Personal liability, fire, storm, theft, farm crops, and automobile insurance plans do not provide annuity payments either, but they are insurance nevertheless. Few (if any) persons take exactly the same amount out of these plans that they put into them.

Social insurance is a form of meeting need before it arises, thus eliminating the necessity for many forms of public assistance. It promotes self-respect and dignity, making it unnecessary for many aged or disabled persons to come to their families or to public or private welfare agencies begging for help.

The total cost of protection is much less to the individual under social insurance than it would if he were to provide equivalent means of covering his own risks. At first glance this statement may seem to be an error, but it is true. All people are faced with the risks which are covered, but fortunately only a relatively small number are overtaken by catastrophes. Retirement needs are fully predictable for the total group covered. The labor force is growing, so the increase in persons drawing from the system during retirement is more than compensated for by the increased number paying into the system. Basing benefits upon automatic eligibility standards rather than means saves a vast amount of investigative effort and thus saves money. There is no need for competitive advertising and no salesmen's commissions to pay at the time of registration. There is but one master set of records, so the duplication and overlapping that would occur through taking out numerous private policies for specific types of risks is avoided.

Equivalent protection under private profit-making commercial insurance plans would cost much more, for those who do not expect to collect would not be likely to take out policies. On the other hand, those whose needs are greatest often have the lowest and least certain incomes and therefore cannot afford to take out private insurance. Without social insurance the costs of public assistance would be much higher.

It is the author's opinion that Christians ought to work for the extension of social insurance programs. They stave off many welfare needs and pay the costs of others in our complex, industrialized, capitalistic society. They meet the welfare needs of people in a framework of human dignity and respect. They base benefits upon what a person has done, not upon what he has failed to do. They serve people better than the alternatives of either completely voluntary private social services or public assistance programs.

Until a better, realistically attainable alternative means of meeting such needs is proposed, social insurance seems to be the practical program that is nearest to the "Christian ideal." It does not demand that anyone carry the badge of economic inadequacy; it preserves the self-respect of even the poor. The expansion of the social insurance provisions of the Social Security Act since 1935 gives testimony to the general satisfaction that surrounds it.

Social security represents the entire community working together to meet common needs, not one part of the community caring for another in an attitude of condescending pity or contempt. It thus promotes self-reliance and incentive. Public assistance will always be necessary as a supplement to social insurance, but whenever the two become alternative means to solve the same type of problem, social insurance is preferable.

Churches ought to help raise the standards of public assistance and social insurance programs. They should work for the elimination of inequitable and unkind policies and should promote good administrative procedures.

When there are abuses in any welfare system, Christians should correct them. This does not necessarily mean that they should take steps to eliminate the entire system because it is imperfect. The alternatives — with their actual and potential imperfections — must be a part of their consideration.

Christian love is revealed in a wide variety of "secular" contexts as well as in church-related programs and activities. It includes extending the range of services which will prevent dependency and help dependent people become self-supporting, self-respecting citizens.

Community Action

Many churches are confused about their relationship to community life. This confusion is not a result of ambiguities in the Bible. Instead it results from a failure to make biblical teachings relevant to the twentieth century.

Some Christian leaders have dwelt upon the churches' "sins of commission" in relationship to community life. More significant in most churches are the "sins of omission." Many churches have lost their community perspective, their concern for community problems, and their recognition of the close connections between community progress and congregational welfare. As a result, local churches

> have been transformed into more or less selective little fellowships, frequently composed of people recruited from but a single stratum in the class system. As this transformation has occurred, a narrow-minded parochialism has cast its shadow over the life of one urban congregation after another. More and more the average Christian congregation has come to be concerned with its own little program and with its own membership (or prospective membership) .[2]

Some churches are organized for action at nearly every social level — individual behavior, family life, politics, international relations, home and foreign missions, etc. — except that of the community. The need for community action is apparent whenever one recognizes that the gospel is concerned with the whole man. Churches alone cannot meet all the needs of man, but their moral insights and spiritual guidance can greatly improve community action on every level.

The effects of family problems, alcoholism, mental illness, juvenile delinquency, unemployment, race relations, war, and all other social problems are evident most clearly in the local community. Here is an open door for churches cooperating through ministerial associations, evangelical alliances, or church

[2] Gerhard E. Lenski, Jr., "The Church and Community Change," *The City Church*, XII (Jan.-Feb., 1962) , 7.

councils, as well as through their individual members and sub-groups like men's brotherhoods. They can visit leaders in local government and community agencies to assure them of prayerful Christian support for their burden of responsibility. They can propose and help to develop policies to meet the needs of all people. They can establish programs to meet needs previously ignored. They can reveal new needs through research and study groups. They can educate members and others to support the law and promote human welfare. They can rally support for wholesome social reforms. They can find and prepare volunteers for needed services. They can recruit youth for relevant occupational roles. They can furnish religious services of spiritual counseling, chaplaincies, Bible study groups, and worship to agencies which cannot minister directly to man's religious needs. They can cooperate in community improvement projects as a demonstration of Christian concern. They can help people in the church and community see the direct relevance of the Christian gospel to practical details of living together in a community.

Such activities may be led by the social action committees of local churches. They will have evangelistic and educational results as well as a preventive and therapeutic effect upon social problems. They will lift the entire community socially and morally. By promoting God's Kingdom in its own community, the church, like its individual members, proves itself to be neighbor to men who are in need (Luke 10:36).

Problems of Church-Society Relationships

Many difficulties arise when the church deals with secular institutions and agencies. Some representative problems will be sketched in this section.

1. *The competing demands of religious ideals and secular interests pose a major dilemma.* In order to have influence in the community, a church must have a strong and influential membership, but in order to increase membership significantly, it must reduce its qualifications for membership unless it is in a rapidly growing community or is favored by other exceptional circumstances. As Yinger has demonstrated, the struggle for power thus may lead a church to adopt secular disciplinary measures, permit the invasion of secular interests, and compromise some

135

of its idealistic purity. Insistence upon strict obedience to a set of values, beliefs, and standards for conduct usually causes loss of power in society, for it typically is associated with small numbers.[3]

Part of the solution to this problem may be to eliminate standards of "purity" which are man-made and not an essential part of the gospel. It also is important to recognize that influence is not necessarily related directly to the size of a congregation, for influence usually is mediated through persons who have leadership abilities or are good participants in committee work. A small church blessed with many such persons using their opportunities in community agencies, commissions, and study groups is apt to wield far more power than a large church with few such members or none. There are enough exceptions to the general pattern of growth only through lowering membership qualifications to prove that this is not an inescapable dilemma. Nevertheless, church leaders must be aware of this problem and tread a careful course in their efforts to increase both the purity and the influence of their church.

2. *Christians tend to become conformed to the world.* Perhaps as a result of their emphasis upon the personal nature of religious conversion, evangelicals are often blind to the social implications of the gospel. They tend to insist upon maintaining the social order, which easily leads to a sanctifying of the status quo as "Christian." But present society is not perfect. When Christians oppose any and all change, when they see virtue only in the political and economic goals of the rich, they actually support a "gospel of wealth." By assuming that everything in America is "Christian," they patriotically hallow national goals that may injure or deprive a majority of God's image-bearers on earth.

It is very evident that the atheistic policies and propaganda of the Soviet Union and Communist China are attacks on Christianity. But other attacks take subtler forms. There is the pseudo-religious doctrine of scientism, which preaches that science has all the answers to the problems of men. There is also the popular doctrine that the church is outmoded and irrelevant

---

[3] See J. Milton Yinger, *Religion in the Struggle for Power* (Durham, N. C.: Duke University Press, 1946), for further elaboration of this problem.

in modern industrial society. But the attack upon Christianity may also invade the church as a sinful leaven which stresses wealth, occupational prestige, and other materialistic standards for evaluating church people and institutions. It may even hide under a mask of personal piety which cannot withstand subtle societal attacks upon Christian faith and principles.

Christians can withstand these pressures to be conformed to the world only by great effort. Promoting the changes that move society in the direction of Christian goals for human welfare will help.

3. *Modern mass society poses special problems of ethics.* Citizens of the modern free world live under governments which rest on the consent of the governed. Such governments are greatly different from the Roman Empire in which the New Testament was written. What is the moral responsibility of the contemporary citizen for the misdeeds of his government, a government "of the people"? To what extent are citizens of the United States accountable before God for the injustices suffered by American Indians, for the cruelty and deprivation foisted upon Japanese-Americans during their relocation in World War II, and for the atomic bombs dropped on Hiroshima and Nagasaki? If a citizen or a church fails to participate in political processes to prevent and protest corruption in government, does he not share in the moral blame attached to these evils? If he votes in ignorance of a candidate's record of self-gratification and opportunism, fails to correct faulty legal procedures, does not seek reparations for those who have been unjustly treated by government, or simply performs his duties with no thought of their ethical significance, is he not as much at fault as was Adolf Eichmann, who simply carried out orders in the genocide of World War II which saw millions of Jews murdered? No action *is* action — and usually it is action in support of evil.

Christians condemn selfishness. Yet they are so caught up in the spirit of the age that their political and economic behavior as members of labor unions, chambers of commerce, professional associations, business corporations, farmers' organizations, and political parties is dominated by a selfishness that seeks the greatest possible benefits for themselves. They rationalize that what's best for their own group is best for everyone. Why should the selfish policies of a group be any less unethical than the selfishness of an individual? The chief decisions of modern society are made in small groups which formulate policies, draw up contrasts, and establish principles. Christians have an increasingly significant role to play in studying and evaluating the morality of group conduct if their religion is to remain relevant.

4. *Abuses in political life, welfare programs, and community activities should be overcome*. Don't let them overcome you! There are flaws in every system of services and in every administration thereof, but this does not by itself imply that they should be abandoned. Public assistance programs sometimes are operated by inadequately qualified personnel, but so are businesses, schools, and even churches. "Chiselers" and cheaters are found in all economic groups, not solely among the recipients of welfare services. Much of the waste that pervades government contract work is caused by abuses in the private companies that do the work. If we reject a government program because it contains imperfections, we ought to be consistent and reject our educational, religious, and economic systems as well, for none of them is perfect either.

If we try to correct evil by throwing out every imperfect service, we will be confronted with even greater evils than we had before we began our "corrective" work. It is far better to hold fast that which is good while we abstain from evil and try to eliminate the abuses of basically wholesome institutions and practices. A balanced perspective will see the values of a system as well as its flaws.

5. *Church-state relationships pose special problems*. Religious institutions as such ought to be cared for by the people whose religion they promote. But when a church-sponsored agency provides social services to citizens in general and devotes only a relatively small part of the total program to its unique religious message and activities, many believe it is entitled to the receipt of surplus food or other subsidies from the government. Where the line between church and state ought to be drawn in welfare work is one of the current controversies over the interpretation of federal and state constitutions. Christians need to give this question careful and realistic attention.

Many relevant questions can be asked. Is it valid for the state to "deputize" religious agencies to perform welfare tasks which are increasingly considered a role of government and then to subsidize these agencies with government funds? The care of the aged, dependent children, tuberculosis patients, the mentally ill and mentally deficient, and other dependent people is primarily a concern of the total society, not of the church alone; is it not therefore valid to use tax funds to support such church-sponsored services as long as such funds are not directly used to support chaplains, religious instruction, and indoctrination? Is religious liberty violated by such practices? Is it necessary to draw a line of separation between church and state in the welfare services of our society?

It is easy to be inconsistent in political behavior. We may condemn in others what we praise or condone in ourselves. If we think it is wrong for Catholics to use a given kind of influence or pressure, it is not right for us to use that same type of pressure. If it is wrong in our pluralistic society for public schoolteachers to use Islamic, Buddhist, Jewish, or Catholic prayers in the public school classroom, we ought not to introduce Protestant prayers. If we do not want another religious group to be "the power behind the throne," we should not seek that position for ourselves in local, state, or national politics. Religious liberty for ourselves and the separation of other churches from the state necessitates consistent, exemplary conduct on our own part.

6. *Cooperation with other religious groups may create problems.* Enough has been said on this in previous chapters. Every situation is different, so each needs to be considered in its own right.

7. *It is difficult to balance idealism and realism.* Church leaders tend to emphasize ideals so much that it is often difficult for their members to choose among alternatives which are neither purely ideal nor clearly wicked. Practical choices are usually between admixtures of good and evil. It is difficult for Christians to act when every possible choice necessitates the acceptance of imperfections which seem to be or are sinful.

Although heaven is impossible on earth, the insights of heaven can inform and influence decisions. Christians should help one another in these choices so that the goal of promoting

139

God's Kingdom is constantly before them as an objective. Love should be the aim, but it should be tempered with the realization that "perfect love" will never be present in *all* Christians in this life, and much less so in all people of scciety. To uphold it as if it were an attainable goal is highly unrealistic.

8. *Some assume that expanding social legislation is a result of Christian failure.* They believe that the church should have practiced what it preaches about love; if it had not failed to do the job, "the world" would not have stepped in. We have already seen that conditions of modern society, plus the fact that dedicated Christians are only a minority of its population, make that conclusion inconsistent with the facts. The scope of problems is too great for the church to meet them all. Furthermore, Christian values have helped to introduce many of the welfare services offered through government.

9. *The church must avoid the biases of other groups.* It is easy to see how *others* have falsely assumed that the values of certain parts of the population were Christian; it is difficult to discern how we ourselves are bound by similar biases. The political, economic, and social judgments of every special interest group, no matter how competent and honest its members may be, should be examined carefully instead of being accepted as "the whole truth" on any issue.

Even though it seeks to be the "conscience of society," the church itself needs constructive criticism. It must evaluate and re-evaluate its basic goals in the light of the Scriptures and the changing realities of the world. It must beware of becoming the tool of unscrupulous elements of the community which seek to exploit it. It must recognize that eagerly provided "scriptural" rationalizations may lead to evil when applied to social action programs. The church must never become the instrument of vested interests in society. It must remain independent, subservient only to Jesus Christ as He leads through the Holy Spirit and the Holy Scriptures.

An exchange of ideas, insights, and experiences with representatives of churches in other societies can help Christians correct each other. An intermingling of members of different occupations, social classes, and interests in the same congregation can help them to keep every economic system and political perspective under the judgment of God. Theological scholarship can help to prevent the misuse of "theological principles" to justify the policies of a special interest group.

Every political and economic system is open to criticism at some points; at other points they may be consistent with the demands of Christian stewardship. After all, Romans 13 was written to Christians under a government that we would call a dictatorship!

10. *Maintaining a wholesome perspective is not easy.* Today, as in the days of Jesus, it is easy to "strain at a gnat and swallow a camel" (Matt. 23:24). We readily enter into traditional programs of attacking the evils of alcohol, but it is difficult to become concerned about the destructive potential of H-bombs and nuclear fallout. We are quick to condemn premature marriages necessitated by pregnancy, but slow to concern ourselves with those basic conditions in modern urban society and unhealthy emphases in mass communications which stimulate unrealistic expectations from sex. We find it easy to attack divorce but hard to face realistically the social changes which have furthered it.

It is wise to stop occasionally to take an over-all view of society and its problems, evaluating which are primary and which are secondary. Social science reports and interpretations can be very helpful to this task. Church action should give as much or more attention to basic causes of human suffering as it does to the symptoms of personal need which result.

Conclusion

We no longer live in a medieval society where church and state unitedly lord it over human lives. The church nevertheless has a role to play in society if it will but accept its great opportunities in a spirit of meekness, lest it, too, be tempted and led astray. The indispensable basis for all of its witness is the Bible. Theological principles derived from Scripture and enlightened by centuries of experience in the Christian church are very important. Careful checks upon a church to determine whether it is truly seeking God's will and not merely institutional advancement are also helpful.

We have no control over whether Christ's return will be at the beginning, middle, or end of a great tribulation, but we can help to control what occurs in society meanwhile. Those who belong to Him will purify themselves (I John 3:3). They cannot purify themselves without also purifying a society that otherwise will continue to corrupt them and other people. Social action must take its rightful place in the church of Jesus Christ.

As the church prayerfully seeks to speak the truth in love and to act as a humble, even suffering, servant, it will be given the wisdom of God for its prophetic witness and social service tasks.

SUGGESTIONS FOR DISCUSSION AND STUDY

1. How might the statement, "The Christian is in the world, but not of the world," be misinterpreted? How does this cause a distortion of the Christian witness?

2. If a church becomes involved in the practical problems of its community, it may find compromise necessary and thus lose some of its Christian purity. If it refuses to compromise, it may cut itself off from all community influence and as a result "let the world go to the devil." How can Christians resolve this dilemma?

3. If a social agency, service club, or community center supports many activities that a church approves, but also another activity of which the church disapproves, how should the church relate itself to that agency? What should its members do in relationship to it? How is this problem similar to the dilemma of political action?

4. Why have formal welfare services expanded so greatly during this century? Have they increased in your own community? How? Why? Should Christians resist or encourage the expansion of government welfare services? Why? How?

5. Compare your denomination's resolutions about social welfare and social action with the implementation of these resolutions in its congregations in your community. Are some emphasized and others ignored? Why? What ought to be done about situations of this kind?

6. What service projects are sponsored or promoted by organizations in your community like the League of Women Voters, Jaycees, Kiwanis Club, Lion's Club, Rotary, Better Business Bureau, American Legion, fraternal orders, labor unions, YMCA, and gospel missions? Ought your church or its members to become involved in any of these projects? Why or why not?

7. To what extent does your community depend upon outside sources for its food, shelter, clothing, manufactured goods, markets for its products, books and magazines, radio and television programs, education, and other goods and services? What does the growing interdependence of everybody in a complex society imply for social welfare and social action?

8. Identify some basic social reforms that have occurred in the history of your community. What role did Christians play in those reforms? Were churches involved as organizations? How? With what effects? If any churches refused to take a stand on the issues, did they thereby help one side in the controversy? What were the results?

9. Identify the primary sources of income in your community. Are the basic decisions that determine the policies of these industries and businesses made by individual persons, a local board of directors, government, or a board of control that is located in a distant city? What does this imply for your community? Has it implications for local, state, and federal governments and for church action?

10. Divide into small groups of not more than four or five persons each and visit the following agencies in your community: County Welfare Office; Criminal Court; Juvenile Court; Domestic Relations Court; Public Health Office; U. S. or State Employment Service; Vocational Rehabilitation Center; Mental Health Clinic (or mental hospital, or psychiatric clinic); Red Cross; Council of Social Agencies (or United Fund, or Community Chest). What services are provided by each? What special problems do they face? What unmet needs do their workers identify in your community? What is the Christian response to these unmet needs?

143

RECOMMENDED READING

Barnes, Roswell P., *Under Orders*. Garden City, N. Y.: Doubleday, 1961. An analysis of the role of Christian churches in public affairs, which are defined as "all the interests of the community as a whole and the social forces that impinge upon persons." Includes examples of types of activity by which churches exert influence.

Bennett, John C., *Christian Ethics and Social Policy*. New York: Scribner's, 1946. A survey and critique of five strategies for relating Christian ethics to public social issues.

Christian Life Commission Pamphlets, Baptist General Convention of Texas, 703 North Ervay, Dallas, Texas. Six series of attractive pamphlets on the Bible in relationship to social issues, the application of Christian principles, problems of teen-agers, family problems, Christian counseling, and Christianity and Communism.

Danzig, David, "The Radical Right and the Rise of the Fundamentalist Minority," *Commentary*, XXXIII (April, 1962), 291-298. A description and analysis of relationships between Christian fundamentalism and right-wing extremism.

Maston, T. B., *The Christian in the Modern World*. Nashville, Tenn.: Broadman Press, rev. ed., 1955. An evangelical leadership training book on what it means to be a Christian in the modern world.

Obenhaus, Victor, *The Responsible Christian*. Chicago: University of Chicago Press, 1957. A Protestant interpretation for laymen on the role Christians must play in the economic and social world if the Christian faith is not to lose its vitality.

Chapter 8

Christian Vocations and Social Concern

Now ye are the body of Christ, and members in particular.

And God hath set some in the church, first apostles, secondarily prophets, thirdly teachers, after that miracles, then gifts of healings, helps, governments, diversities of tongues (I Cor. 12:27-28).

As every man hath received the gift, even so minister the same one to another, as good stewards of the manifold grace of God (I Pet. 4:10).

BECAUSE RELIGION IS SO OFTEN THOUGHT TO BE "ONLY" FOR THE spiritual side of life, people typically feel that it has nothing to do with their politics, economic perspectives, recreation, and daily work. This type of thinking is not limited to nonchristians and theologically liberal Christians. It is very common among evangelicals as well — perhaps even more common.

In some such churches "only the Bible" is taught; this leads to a focus upon the "spiritual" lessons of the Scriptures. Applying the Bible to daily activities seems to be a means of trying to earn salvation by good works. On the Sunday before Labor Day, and only then, church services may be devoted especially to the subject of work, but even these will focus typically on secondary details pertaining to work habits and the evangelism of fellow workers.

Such perspectives have indirectly promoted the opinion that one's spiritual life has little to do with his daily work, provided only that he is in an honorable vocation, is honest, and does not swear when things go wrong. Christian morality is identified with the demands of a religious institution rather than with the demands of one's occupation, except as the latter provides the income which he can tithe! Fortunately, however, there are signs that these fallacies are losing ground.

The Importance of Work

Work has many meanings. Some Christians have viewed it as a necessary evil, a curse put upon mankind as a result of sin (Gen. 3:19). Some have seen it as an activity for which God ultimately will give religious rewards; one gains spiritual status and assures himself of being among the elect by success in his work. Some consider work to be a means of securing income, status, or power over other people. Others view it as an intrinsically meaningful activity; craftsmanship and other satisfying experiences in work are their own reward. Still others view work as a means to gain time and income, which in turn they can use to please God or else please themselves.

Work in the modern world is often regarded as the dreariest part of one's existence. Consuming is fun; producing is drudgery. When a person goes to his job he is selling a piece of himself, so that he may enjoy the rest of his time. His occupational label is like a price tag: it tells his worth in terms of prestige or social status.

Work gives men their self-images. It places them in a social context, and in this context they are appraised by others. It is the source of economic livelihood. It is an index to political views and a key to much social and recreational life. More than any other one aspect of men's behavior, work makes them what they are. Work is also one of the most important bases for people's economic level of living, place of residence, recreational habits, friendships, and other activities. Church programs and personal social and recreational experiences, for example, must be adjusted to the work routines of people, not vice versa.

Work is far more important in the Bible, theology, and Christian living than the typical church program is likely to reveal.

A Christian View of Work

The words translated "work" in the Bible have many different meanings. (Compare Phil. 2:12-13 with Exod. 20:9;

146

Eccl. 12:14; Isa. 2:8; and John 6:28 for examples.) Yet there is an underlying perspective which deserves much attention.

The very first picture of God is that of a worker busy at the task of creation. "In the beginning God created the heaven and the earth" (Gen. 1:1). To man, the crown of creation, God gave the work of subduing the earth, holding dominion over every living thing, and dressing and keeping the garden of Eden (Gen. 1:28-31; 2:15). Work thus preceded the fall of man. It was an aspect of man's being created in the image of God, the Divine Worker who sanctifies work by His own example.

Jesus Christ, God Incarnate, was a worker. He worked during the early years of His life, most likely as a carpenter, and He continued to work the works of His heavenly Father throughout His earthly ministry (John 5:36; 9:4; etc.). He continues to hold all things together (Col. 1:17) and to serve as a "merciful and faithful high priest" working to help those who are tempted (Heb. 2:17-18).

Both the nature and the example of God thus sanctify work. Man as a planner and executor of plans is imitating God. All property belongs to God, so all work with property is an aspect of stewardship. Work is not merely an activity undertaken for the purpose of providing a means for subsistence. It is a sacred duty to which God calls men, a status in which God uses men to glorify Him.

The Lordship of Christ over every area of life includes work. Since the Christian gospel is concerned with the whole man, it is vitally concerned with man's daily work as well as his personal devotions, family life, and church activities. In his daily work man serves his fellow men and God. The interdependence of all people is so great that there is no truly independent, self-made man. He who proclaims his own accomplishments the loudest is helpless without the products of other people, the language received from past generations, the education given him in childhood, the market provided by others for his goods and services, and innumerable additional contributions from his fellow men. In a tangible, material way as well as in regard to spiritual influence, "none of us liveth to himself, and no man dieth to himself" (Rom. 14:7).

God calls men to salvation, but He also calls men to serve.

147

(Compare I Cor. 1:26; 7:17-24; Eph. 1:18; 4:1, 4; II Thess. 1:11; Heb. 3:1; and II Pet. 1:10 with Rom. 12:4-8; I Cor. 12:4-31; and I Pet. 4:10-11.) God has given each man abilities and opportunities as He wills. These are to be used for the common good of all, not for mere selfish gain.

Thus the Christian doctrine of work is focused upon God more than upon work. God personally encounters each man in his actual situation and is concerned about his daily life at work as well as in church. At all times the center of life for the Christian should be his relationship with God. He should recognize that all of life is sacred, and that every moment he can help fulfill the Great Commission of Christ to go into all the world — including his place of work — with the gospel.

Meaningful work is a service of love to one's neighbor. Its products and services contribute to the well-being of others. The rivet in an airplane, the statistic in an accountant's records, the stitch in a shoe sole, the words in a book, the assuring smile of a social worker, the hole in a computer's punch card, and the spoon delivered by a waitress — all of these can minister both to the bodies and the spirits of one's fellow men.

The Christian who is subject to the Lordship of Christ in his daily work is the most significant emissary of the Christian gospel to the whole world. Every Christian layman is in this sense a minister of Christ; this ministry is his basic "other vocation."[1] He is a partner with God in his daily work. What happens in church buildings during week ends is important, but it is far less important to the Kingdom of God than that which occurs on the working days of the week.

The daily work of every faithful Christian is a *vocation*, an occupation to which he has been called by God to serve Him by serving his fellow men. Even monotonous daily routines become avenues of joyful service to those who have heard God's call. They no longer perform them as meaningless and empty drudgeries, perfunctorily, carelessly, and as quickly as possible, for they know their contributions promote the work of God and the good of mankind.

Most jobs also provide opportunities to associate with other people, to make friends with them, and to show oneself sym-

[1] Elton Trueblood, *Your Other Vocation* (New York: Harper, 1952).

148

pathetic and helpful in their times of personal need. A positive life of consistent service to God at one's work will give many opportunities to witness to His grace that otherwise would never come to the Christian (I Pet. 3:15).

Vocational Choice

One of the most significant ways in which a church can serve God is to inspire its members to choose their occupations in a truly Christian manner, making them *vocations* in the fullest sense of that word. Every church should so inspire its young people through Sunday school programs, sermons, discussion groups, young people's meetings, and other techniques. If the choice of vocation is made on selfish grounds, it becomes an enduring sin, for this is a deliberate withholding of allegiance from God in a major area of life which conditions all other aspects of life. And if some church member who has made this kind of mistake in the past now recognizes this fact, the church can help him find a more satisfactory alternative. It can support him morally and spiritually even if the change is "a step down" by worldly standards.

There are certain principles which the church should follow in providing vocational guidance. It should stress basic Christian values of stewardship and commitment to Christ, for example. It should warn against occupations which harm others. It should commend for special consideration that work which can be done by Christians only. No one but the church will make great efforts to recruit religious educators, missionaries, evangelists, pastors, and chaplains, but professional and educational organizations of many types sponsor recruitment campaigns for other occupations.

Everyone has a different combination of abilities and interests. God will not call a person into a vocation for which he lacks the minimum qualifications. He may, however, call him to a job which requires a program of education or vocational training. The abilities and endowments which God has given an individual can be determined through psychological tests and vocational aptitude scales, which are available from high-school and college counselors and employment agencies. As a general rule (there may be exceptions) a person possessing unusual abilities should not use them in occupations which can be filled

149

by almost anyone. God will seldom call the ten-talent man to a one-talent job unless, perhaps, He wishes to develop that man's character and his understanding of others for bigger future tasks.

The faithful Christian's incentive in vocational choice will go far beyond economic considerations and social status goals. Like the heroes of old (Heb. 11), he will experience the adventure of faith by going God's way, even if this way leads to longer hours of work for a lower income in a "despised" social status.

In my opinion God will not call one into a vocation without giving him a driving interest in it. The Christian who lives faithfully for his God will be given a basic liking for his work, even though every job undoubtedly has some duties that are not appealing.

Need is also relevant to vocational choice. The needs of the Christian church and those of society in general can help Christians to see occupational gaps that should be filled. Some needs can be met only by Christians. Others are more likely to be filled by Christians than by nonchristians because of the nature of their rewards. For instance, social work and the other helping professions are currently experiencing a shortage of personnel. One reason, probably, is the fact that most people prefer jobs with higher pay or more prestige.

Christian love usually can be demonstrated most actively by entering church-related vocations or service occupations like social work, psychiatry, clinical counseling, corrections, public health services, child guidance, and institutional administration, to mention but a few. Christians who have been endowed by God with the basic qualifications for such professions ought to give prayerful consideration to them.

Christians likewise should enter the occupations which exercise significant leadership in society. Many of the compromises that are essential in practical politics are distasteful to conscientious Christians, but society will not improve without the active participation of Christians in the legislative, administrative, and judicial branches of government. The labor movement, industry, and business similarly are not likely to adopt more humane practices unless Christians, together with other religious people with high ethical values, influence them in a practical way through sound leadership.

Examples of Christian Vocations

A list of all the vocations Christians ought to consider would be nearly as lengthy as the *Dictionary of Occupational Titles* published by the U. S. Government Printing Office. It is neither necessary nor justifiable to list thousands of jobs here, so attention will be called to only a few representative occupations which are especially worthy of consideration by Christian youth. This does not imply that others are not equally important.

The vocations mentioned here are especially relevant to Christian social responsibilities. Many of them are relatively little publicized in most churches. The brief suggestions in this chapter can be supplemented by Christian education publications, theological seminary recruitment materials, public relations information from Christian colleges, data from vocational counselors, reports of state and federal employment agencies, pamphlets from professional associations, and other sources.

In the modern urban world many people are lonely even though they associate daily with others. Many cannot find satisfying friendships. The "helping professions" which minister directly to individual needs are often called upon to supply the friendship which is otherwise lacking. Much of the pastoral work of the clergyman is devoted to being a friend to relatively isolated and lonely people. The average medical doctor has several patients who come to him more because of their need for a friend than for physical needs. Marriage counselors find that many of their clients have not learned how to be friends in the full sense. Psychiatrists, clinical psychologists, and psychiatric social workers have many clients whose basic need is for friends. These modern professions which offer psychotherapy, especially psychiatry, can actually be viewed from the perspective of selling friendship.[2] Christians in these occupations have a tremendous opportunity to serve people and influence them in ways that will promote the goals of society and the Kingdom of Christ.

Rehabilitation services of many kinds need personnel. Medical doctors, nurses, physical therapists, occupational therapists, speech pathologists, speech and hearing therapists, rehabilitation coun-

---

2 See William Schofield, *Psychotherapy: The Purchase of Friendship* (Englewood Cliffs, N. J.: Prentice-Hall, 1946).

selors, music therapists, and medical social workers often co-operate in rehabilitation teams to restore lost or impaired abilities to those who have been injured by accidents, diseases, or other disabilities. Special teachers for the handicapped and mentally retarded are similarly needed. These all train patients to live and to work within the limits of their disabilities to the fullest extent of their capacities. They use a wide variety of devices and techniques, depending upon their specialty, to help despairing people lead independent and useful lives. Their services are often supplemented by the work of volunteers who give of their free time.

Even those who are unable to get a college education may become qualified for certain helping vocations. Licensed practical nurses who can serve on a visiting nurse basis in the homes of chronically ill patients are greatly needed. There is a short supply of understanding house parents who can demonstrate love to residents of homes for children, schools for the mentally retarded, and correctional institutions for juvenile delinquents. Homemakers who can take charge of a household during the illness or absence of a mother, housewives who can give a foster home to isolated elderly people, and other dedicated helpers are needed in many communities.

Public health nurses work in schools and community agencies. They try to teach people the principles of health and motivate them to change their health habits while they are meeting immediate physical needs. Their task is largely an educational one. They teach people concretely, by demonstrations and example, more than by words.

Hospital administrators are responsible for the physical plant, equipment, coordination of services, finances, public relations, and personnel. They comprise a growing profession which plays a key role in community welfare.

Professional counselors in schools, colleges, rehabilitation agencies, hospitals, industries, and private clinics help people to know their personality assets and guide them in making choices about their education, vocation, job opportunities, and problems. Some of them specialize in vocational rehabilitation, others in marriage counseling. Ministers of the gospel spend much of their pastoral ministry in counseling people who have problems, and much of the work of the military chaplain is devoted to similar tasks. The specialized professions of marriage and family counseling, clinical psychology, and even personnel work in industry use the skills of counseling more than perhaps any other occupation.

Labor-relations work in industry, foreign service jobs with the U.S. Department of State, elective political offices, many public service posts under civil service, police work, youth services in boys' and girls' organizations, and medical technology are other positions in which service is given directly to people as individuals. Opportunities for Christian humanitarian service also are great in such occupations as that of the architect, banker, biologist, businessman, chemist, city planner, dentist, dietitian, engineer, farmer, home economist, journalist, lawyer, librarian, mathematician, mass communications specialist (newspapers, radio, television, etc.), pharmacist, public relations expert, recreational leader, secretary, and traffic manager.

The Christian church should be represented through its members in those occupations which give direct welfare aid and personal assistance to people in need. It must also be represented in other occupations which make the basic decisions in society that either cause, cure, or prevent welfare needs. Real estate developers, contractors, business administrators, industrial executives, labor leaders, lawyers, politicians, news analysts and commentators, university professors, and research scientists all help to make the world what it is becoming. Christians should be on the front lines of policy formulation as well as in the middle and rear echelons of relatively routine implementation and work. Only thus will they be able to make the greatest possible impact for Christ and for the welfare of all mankind.

One of the broadest and most representative of the many vocations which are devoted directly to helping people in need is social work. Evangelicals in general avoided it in the pre-World War II era, perhaps because it seemed too closely allied to the social gospel and to liberal theologies that focused solely upon temporal affairs. Nevertheless, social work deserves special attention because its principles of service have a general application to all efforts to help people.

Social Work

Professional social work has its roots in the deeds of mercy and acts of charity which have been associated historically with the Judeo-Christian religion. One of the very first developments in the history of the Christian church was the setting apart of lay officers to minister to the daily needs of widows (Acts 6:1-6). "Ministry" is a spiritual gift specifically referred to in the New Testament; it was probably exercised primarily in meeting physical and material needs (Rom. 12:7; I Pet. 4:11). These services were expanded rapidly and systematically, as many portions of the New Testament show. The clearest of these is I Timothy 5:3-16, which gives regulations for the registration of widows receiving church aid.

Social work emerged out of the historical background of private and especially church-related welfare. Friendly visiting by church members, food baskets, poor funds, deacons' benevolent funds, and pastoral services are a few of the church activities which preceded modern social work. Foundling homes, hospitals, other welfare agencies, and a host of social reforms in Western civilization on both sides of the Atlantic are also a part of the historical background of modern social work.

Almost all people have needs at some period in their lives for which skilled social work help is needed, just as they need professional, medical, legal, and spiritual help at times. It takes competence as well as compassion to lead people to adopt new ideas and practices that will enrich their own lives and make them a blessing rather than a burden to society. This competence is developed in professional training for social work.

At its best, social work is a form of love in practice. The fact that this goal is often unattained reflects the immaturity of men, including some social workers, rather than a flaw in the profession's basic philosophy. Social work involves the art and skill of helping people, freeing them and supporting them to develop greater independence. It has the goal of a more abundant life for mankind. It helps others to help themselves.

Social work emphasizes the importance to each person of his being accepted by others, being needed, having meaningful roles in life, and being loved. To accept a person as he is in order to help him is entirely consonant with Christian compassion. Indeed, *agape* love with its charity and compassion is a sustaining motivation for the competent social worker.

Social work presupposes a belief in the worth of the individual which agrees closely with the Christian teaching that man is created in the image of God. A person is respected even when he is "down and out." He, too, enjoys the right to health, freedom from want, an education in accord with his competence, work, civil liberty, and protection if he becomes dependent.

The social worker does not enforce standards of "worthiness" as a prerequisite for assistance, which in effect amount to a requirement that a person will not be aided until he has reformed, no longer needs help, or has proved himself to be the same kind of person as the one who is giving the aid. The social worker begins with people as they are; in this respect he is like Christ, who went to the sick, not to those who were whole. "Means tests" to determine eligibility for public or private welfare assistance are probably unavoidable, but they often demean the persons who receive aid, tear down human dignity, and take away the self-respect of persons created in God's image. There is, of course, always a danger that obnoxious individuals will take unfair advantage of available assistance programs. Careful study reveals, however, that this problem is sometimes caused by other injustices which also need to be corrected.

Social work emphasizes the belief that individuals can grow and change. Such a belief is closely related to the faith of evangelistically minded Christians who know that by God's grace the person who is dead in trespasses and sins can be transformed into "a new creature" in Jesus Christ.

This in turn is closely linked with a belief in the autonomy of the individual — his "free will" or self-determination. Social work emphasizes the right of a person to live his own life as long as he does not harm the rights of others. It encourages people to develop new outlooks, a new philosophy of living which will motivate them to change their own patterns of behavior.

Social work also recognizes the interdependence of all men on the cultural, economic, social, political, and spiritual levels. It helps men to relate themselves more effectively to other men. Beginning with people where they are, accepting them as autonomous beings, and encouraging them to see their own opportunities and responsibilities for change, social workers attempt to develop

new self-concepts in individuals and as a result new patterns of
action. Obviously this takes a combination of knowledge, understanding, and skills that necessitates professional education and
experience. More than just compassion is needed to be an effective social worker!

Through the experience and insights of professional social
work, we know that "deeds of mercy" can reflect a lack of
true brotherly love. Parents or foster parents may use a child to
fill empty spots in their own personalities. People may engage
in social welfare work because they need to prove to themselves
or others that they are better than the recipients of their help.
Such persons can demoralize and pauperize a victim of social
problems rather than help him.

From the long-range perspective, social workers attempt to
conserve public funds. They recognize that a few dollars in taxes
saved today may require the expenditure of a great deal more in
the future. Instead of simply aiding social cripples, social workers
attempt to heal them so that they will arise, take up their social
responsibilities, and walk as dignified contributing members of
society.

Social workers emphasize the essential uniqueness of each individual, the existence of common human needs, and the societal
responsibilities of every person. The well-being of all citizens
is the foundational goal of social work.

The three primary methods of social work are *casework*, helping people on an individual basis; *group work*, helping them
through group activities; and *community organization*, helping
communities meet their health and welfare needs. Supporting
services of administration, research, and social action also provide
opportunities for service in the profession. A wide variety of
specific fields of practice is included in the profession. These
include child welfare, corrections (parole, probation, and institutional services), community planning, settlement houses and
other group service agencies, public assistance, church social
work, family services, medical social work, psychiatric social
work, and school social work.

> For the Christian, Social Work is love made visible through
> the ability of one person to help another in need. It is a service
> to people in need — as individuals, or in groups or communities.
> The goal of Social Work is to help these people function more

156

effectively in today's world. Solutions to individual and social problems are found through helping people help themselves.

. . . The social worker uses his knowledge of both individual and group behavior. He must understand the emotional, social and spiritual needs of the person seeking help and must know the community resources which can be mobilized to assist in providing this help.[3]

The profession of social work is not aimed only at handing out material aid, as is all too commonly thought. It tries to prevent social problems and to alleviate those which have already emerged. Giving material help is only an adjunct to the total casework process. Both preventive and curative work are involved in this significant profession, which many more Christians of both sexes ought to enter.

Some Problems of Christian Vocation

Christians too often get indoctrinated with the materialistic ideologies of their society. As a result, like others they are eager to leave the slums for the prosperous suburbs, so some of the schoolteachers, medical doctors, lawyers, and others who remain in the inner city are among the least capable in their professions. Where human needs are greatest, competence is scarcest, for the highly competent are lured away by rewards of money and social status.

It is true, however, that the person with the highest income and in the most prominent social class often has the greatest influence in society. Christians may seek such status as means to an end. On the other hand, Jesus taught that those who are least will be the greatest. This is a dilemma many Christians face in their vocation.

In certain occupations one also may be faced with the question of whether or not he should work in a directly church-related position. There he will minister to people who are primarily of a given religious background. He will be free to express his religious convictions openly. If he works in a non-church-related institution, he must remain religiously "neutral" in his professional relationships. He may, nevertheless, have an indirect

[3] Public Relations Department, Bethel College, *Toward Social Work: A Helping Profession* (St. Paul, Minn.: Bethel College, 1964), pp. 1, 2.

157

Christian impact that will reach out extensively to nonchristian people. He may also have a higher salary. There is no overarching clear-cut answer to questions of these kinds. God leads each person in His own way.

Many evangelical Christians have thought that one chooses to be a minister or a missionary at a special moment of commitment. Revivalistic meetings have led to many such decisions, but a follow-up of these decisions several years later would reveal that most of them do not materialize in the form originally intended. Crowd psychology may lead an entire group of children or youth to raise their hands or go forward. Personal inadequacy, a desire for recognition, and problems of relationships with others may lead to sincere but misguided action. When persons intending to follow through with their commitment enter college or seminary, it sometimes becomes obvious that they lack the minimum qualifications. Many of them confess that social pressures led them into making the decision and also hinder them from rescinding it, even though they know within themselves that it was not of God.

Linked with this problem is the feeling in many groups that God calls men into the ministry through some divine confrontation of a miraculous or semimiraculous type. When a group stresses this as a qualification, highly qualified persons who desire to serve in church-related vocations may never enter them because they have not seen a vision in the night, heard a literal voice from heaven, or received some other spectacular call.

Actually, God's call into any church-related or other vocation is a process — a process that begins with early childhood experiences, continues through formal education, is influenced by events of daily life, and is directed by a combination of opportunities, occupational needs, personal interests, abilities, and experiences. God is at work in all of these.

Changing the concept of the call from one of momentary decision to one of a lifetime process would be a wholesome and scriptural modification of evangelical tradition. This, of course, is not to imply that God never uses semimiraculous techniques to lead people in their vocational choices. At times He does; ordinarily, however, He is working in less obvious ways to lead His children through life.

An unfortunate implication of many Christian discussions of

vocations is that only church-related occupations involve "full-time Christian service." This conveys the impression that other vocations are, at best, Christian only part of the time. Every Christian who faithfully does his daily work as a servant of Jesus Christ is a full-time Christian servant, whether his task be repairing automobiles, building houses, collecting garbage, doing housework, selling groceries, or scrubbing floors. Yet specifically church-related jobs need special attention in the Christian church, for only the church will speak on their behalf.

The most capable young people are invited to enter a wide variety of professions, so the church also must have an active program to inform them of the needs for ministers, missionaries, and other church-related workers. After all, the message of the Holy Spirit that Paul and Barnabas were called into special missionary duties came to the church (Acts 13:1-3). God does not call the individual person only. He does call all to serve — some in the church as preachers, teachers, administrators, translators, and helpers (I Cor. 12:28), and others in society providing men with food, shelter, clothing, and other needs of life. *All* are called into full-time Christian service, not merely those who are ordained by the church to the gospel ministry.

Conclusion

Churches can promote Christian vocations in several ways. Through their educational work and youth programs they can guide youth into commitments that will lead them into occupations of service. They can help Christians overcome temptations to be conformed to worldly standards of success and to see higher motivations and goals in their workaday lives. They can promote vocational groups in which Christian teachers, laborers, businessmen, and the like will help each other grow in the graces of Christian commitment as applied to their own specific vocations. They can keep stressing the fact that every Christian has a ministry, and that this ministry extends to his daily work as well as to his directly church-related activities. They can draw upon the insights, understandings, and knowledge of members and friends from the various professions to enlarge the vision of all in the congregation so they can see the vast scope of human need and hence of Christian service. They can use the specialized skills of church members in various forms of service projects. It may be more beneficial to the cause of Christ for a social worker, for example, to lead a social welfare project of the church than it would be for him to serve as a deacon or teacher of primary boys. He knows community welfare resources and needs much better than other members.

The relationship of the church to the world will be at its strongest and highest level when all the members sense their vocation — their high calling in Jesus Christ, a calling which includes the occupation which is the chief outlet for their service and the source of their economic livelihood. Every Christian is called into full-time Christian service!

SUGGESTIONS FOR DISCUSSION AND STUDY

1. The New Testament seems to teach that self-seeking is sinful. Is it ever right for a Christian to seek a promotion or other advancement in his work? (Consider the effects of increased social status, higher income, and presumably use of one's abilities at the highest attainable level.) Why do people often look more favorably upon professional ministers who "climb the ladder of success" than upon laymen who climb the social ladder? Ought there to be a difference?

2. What scholarship funds are available in your denomination to help students enter the helping professions and church-related vocations? What are the criteria of eligibility? Have high-school and college-age youth in your church been made aware of these financial aids? In what additional ways does your church indirectly support vocational recruitment and preparation? Think, for example, of Christian education publications, Sunday school lessons, financial support of theological education, and contributions to Christian colleges.

3. List and classify the references to "work" and related terms in the Bible. How often is work viewed as a privilege, punishment, duty to God, and duty to man? Does the Old Testament convey a different impression from the New regarding the nature and meaning of work?

4. What are the predominant perspectives toward work among the people of your church? How do their views compare with

those of others in the community? How do they compare with biblical perspectives?

5. What responsibilities does your church have to your pastor? Compare those listed in your church constitution with those given in such Bible passages as I Corinthians 9:1-15; II Corinthians 8 and 9; Galatians 6:6; I Timothy 5:17-20; and Hebrews 13:16-17. What practical considerations do these imply? How does your church's treatment of its minister, both officially and through gossip, influence youth to enter or to stay out of the professional ministry?

6. Survey several church congregations to discover how many persons from the helping professions are in their membership, both in total numbers and as a percentage of their members. What uses are being made of these highly trained professional people in their local church? Is their leadership respected or rejected? Why?

7. What are churches of your community doing to promote political careers for their members? Do they help candidates for local, state, or national public offices in any way? Do competing candidates for local public office have a forum in your community where they may state their views, clarify their position, answer questions, and present citizens with an intelligent basis for voting? How might this promote intelligent vocational choices by youth?

8. In what ways do nonchristians serve God through their occupations? One way to get into this topic is to trace all the sources of recent additions to the property of your church, materials like Sunday school papers and gasoline used in church work, or food which you and other lay and professional ministers of Christ eat. Include those who produced the raw materials, built the machinery to process them, manufactured their containers, and distributed the raw materials and finished products. How many persons have had a part in equipping you physically, materially, and educationally for your Christian vocation? How many of them do you suppose are Christians?

9. Interview representatives of several professions to discover their experiences with churches and pastors. (Medical doctors, social workers, counselors, clinical psychologists, psychiatrists, lawyers, politicians, teachers, and school administrators might be especially relevant.) Do they have favorable or unfavorable atti-

tudes toward the Christian church? Why? What does this imply about the needs for and opportunities of Christians in these professions?

10. Interview clergymen from several denominations to discover their experiences with professional people in occupations like those listed above. Do they have favorable or unfavorable attitudes toward social workers, psychiatrists, politicians, doctors, etc.? Why? What does this imply about the role of Christians in these vocations? How does it influence vocational guidance?

RECOMMENDED READING

Career Information Pamphlets. New York Life Insurance Co., Box 51, Madison Square Station, New York, N. Y. 10010. A series of pamphlets on specific occupations by outstanding leaders in these occupations, written to help parents guide their children into the best choice of a career.

Johnson, F. Ernest, editor, *Religion and Social Work*. New York: Harper, 1956. A symposium on various subjects relating social work to the Christian and Jewish religions.

"Laborers Into His Harvest." New York: *International Journal of Religious Education*, reprint of the January, 1957, issue, Articles and resources on church-related vocations.

Ockenga, Harold John, "Laborers With God," *Christianity Today*, II (Aug. 18, 1958), 9-12. A discussion of Christian vocation by a prominent evangelical pastor.

Trueblood, Elton, *Your Other Vocation*. New York: Harper, 1952. A stimulating interpretation of the ministry of every Christian, his vocation which cuts across all other occupations.

Wentz, Frederick K., *The Layman's Role Today*. Garden City, N. Y.: Doubleday, 1963. A discussion of the need for "a new layman," his way of life, his ministry in the world, and resources for his ministry.

Winn, Albert Curry, *You and Your Lifework: A Christian Choice for Youth*. Chicago: Science Research Associates, 1963. A Christian vocation guide for local church leaders, a guide to parents, and a study notebook for students of high-school age.

Chapter 9

Volunteer Services

For, brethren, ye have been called unto liberty; only use not liberty for an occasion to the flesh, but by love serve one another.

For all the law is fulfilled in one word, even in this; Thou shalt love thy neighbour as thyself (Gal. 5:13-14).

. . . whosoever will be great among you, let him be your minister;

And whosoever will be chief among you, let him be your servant:

Even as the Son of man came not to be ministered unto, but to minister, and to give his life a ransom for many (Matt. 20:26-28).

ALL PEOPLE HAVE NEEDS WHICH VOLUNTEER SERVICES CAN HELP to satisfy. Some of these needs are obvious and relate primarily to transparent economic, social, and psychological problems, while others are relatively hidden, yet present among even the most privileged members of human society. In the first category are the problems related to family disorganization, economic and social deprivation, mental illness, and other aspects of personal and social disorganization. The loneliness of multitudes of people who have daily associations with others at work or in business contacts is often unrecognized. Sometimes acquaintances awaken with a shock to these needs only when it is too late to help — perhaps when a suicide note is found beside a broken body, or after commitment to a mental institution. Guilt-feelings on such occasions are not an adequate compensation for

163

earlier neglect; they cannot undo the harm that has been done by the withholding of friendship and love.

In a society which provides many of the material needs of people who are in trouble it is easy to assume that their "welfare" receives adequate attention. But human needs go far beyond the material level. When all the costs of living, including professional social and medical services, have been fully met, man still has psychological, social, existential, and spiritual needs which can be satisfied only through direct involvement with other people — people who truly care. Volunteer services are important because they help to meet the needs of people with obvious problems.

Volunteer services are important because they also help to meet the needs of those who are economically and socially privileged. The first Director of the Peace Corps, R. Sargent Shriver, has called attention to the many young people who drop out of college with "campus fatigue." They are confused, devitalized, and lacking in ultimate commitments because they have never learned to be of service to others. People whose lives are impoverished by indifference toward others can be revitalized by participation in volunteer services.

Man needs to *give* love as well as to receive it. Giving up money for charitable fund drives can be a demonstration of love, even as cheerful payment of taxes which will be used for social welfare may be, but by itself this is not sufficient to meet the needs of most people. Giving oneself in service by giving up convenience, time, and perhaps even prestige is often a far more tangible and meaningful demonstration of love than financial contributions. The time which is available for such service has increased significantly in recent decades.

The Increase of Leisure Time

In February, 1964, Willard Wirtz, U. S. Secretary of Labor, declared that machines were pushing people aside from their jobs in the United States at the rate of at least 4,000 every 24 hours. Older workers — those past the age of 45 and especially those past 55 — suffer the most from this development. Employers are reluctant to retrain them for new jobs. They are less likely than younger workers to have had a good educational background upon which to build new learning. They suffer even from pension plans which are based upon lengthy periods of employee contributions.

The extension of machine power to do work formerly done by hand — if done at all! — is not particularly new in the world; it is a process that is at least as old as the Industrial Revolution. But in recent years we have seen a new development — automation. Automation involves the use of electronic computers and mechanical devices to control lengthy processes of production, distribution, and record-keeping. Production processes which once consisted of a series of separate steps have become a continuous flow of activities integrated by transfer machines and directed by computers programmed to make their own decisions and corrections at each stage of the process.

Added to automation is the development of new sources of power, especially nuclear energy. These also reduce the total demand for manpower, contribute to more efficient production, increase output per worker, and either reduce the working week or increase unemployment.

Automation in various forms is moving into every major occupation. Even many significant tasks of medical diagnosis are being performed by computers; in the near future automated diagnosticians will supplement or even replace many medical specialists. The concordance to the Revised Standard Version of the Bible was compiled in a few weeks with a computer, instead of in the years of human time that would otherwise have been required. What the future holds is always unclear to men, but it seems likely that the only reasonable alternative to increasingly widespread unemployment is a shorter working week.

Industrial labor a century ago averaged 72 hours a week on a full-time basis. By 1890 it had been reduced to 60 hours. In 1920 it was 48 hours, and in 1955 less than 40 hours. The reduction in the work week was accompanied by great increases in total production, production per worker, and the level of living of the population in general. Automation will probably contribute to additional reductions in working hours, and thus to an increase in leisure time for the majority of the population. As adjustments are made to its massive impact upon society, many workers will find themselves temporarily or permanently out of work. Some of them will be aided by unemployment compensation. Others will join the ranks of the poverty-stricken whose subsistence is derived from welfare funds of labor unions, other private agencies, and state, federal, and local governments. All of them will have much time available. Will it be used constructively or destructively?

Obstacles to Volunteer Service

Despite the great increase in the amount of time that is left to most people's own discretion after they have met the demands of the work week, many requests for assistance in volunteer programs, including those of the church, are often confronted with the plea, "Sorry, I don't have time." Where does time go? How is time spent?

Much of it is devoted to television. The average television viewer spends five hours a day with the "one-eyed monster." Not only is this a problem in its own right, accounting for an average of thirty-five hours per week, but it also has secondary effects. During his five hours on a typical day, the viewer is barraged with more than ninety commercials. He also is exposed to numerous other advertisements through newspapers, magazines, billboards, third-class mail, and other sources. The average American consumer sees or hears a total of about 1,600 advertisements each day.[1] These stimulate the desire to purchase goods and services and to participate in recreational and other activities for self-satisfaction.

In addition to the pressures of advertising which lead people to purchase previously unwanted or unknown goods and services is the cultural demand to "keep up with the Joneses." As the standard of living for one's social class, occupational status, and residential area climbs, one must increase his own consumption in order to prove that he is successful. The luxuries of one decade thus become the necessities of the next.

These influences make a substantial proportion of people dissatisfied because they cannot have all and do all that they have been stimulated to desire. Social pressures lead many mothers to work outside the home for pay, so they no longer have time for volunteer services in the church and in the community. They

[1] Paul F. Douglass and Robert W. Crawford, in James C. Charlesworth, editor, *Leisure in America* (Philadelphia: American Academy of Political and Social Science, Monograph 4, 1964), pp. 63-64.

also stimulate "moonlighting" (part-time work over and above a regular full-time job), which similarly reduces the time available for helping others.

Most people today deliberately try to avoid involvement in the burdens and cares of others. They "pass the buck" to persons officially charged with specific responsibilities. This division of labor generally is time saving and constructive, but at times it becomes a discouraging detriment to the welfare of society and its members. For instance, we may refuse to give our name as a witness to an automobile accident because we do not wish to risk the need to take time out to give testimony in a court trial. When people have financial needs, we assume that welfare funds will help them, not recognizing that it may take three or four weeks before the money comes. When people have problems related to mental health, we label them as "queer" and avoid associations with them. When the physically weak need help with household affairs or other problems, we assume that they can purchase help or that their relatives will provide it. We may even be like the thirty-eight or more persons who saw or heard a woman assaulted in the Kew Garden suburb of New York City early in 1964 and ignored her cries for help.

A wide variety of psychological devices and social evasions help us to wash our hands of responsibility for using some of our time, money, energy, and material possessions to help another who is in need. Despite the increased time at our own disposal, we forget to "bear one another's burdens" (Gal. 5:2) and claim, in effect, that we are not our brothers' keepers.

Churches as well as social welfare agencies and other constructive institutions must face these barriers to volunteer services courageously. Only by overcoming them will the "abundant life" flow to both the "needy" whose problems are obvious and the "prosperous" whose dissatisfactions and lack of happiness stem basically from self-centered greed.

Needed Volunteer Services

The need for voluntary work — work in which one participates of his own free choice without any monetary reward — grows greater daily as society becomes ever more complicated and impersonal. Meaningful social contacts can be provided only on a locally administered and individually tailored basis. Large-scale social services are needed, but they must be supplemented by a new frontier of small-scale local services to individual persons on a face-to-face basis.

Volunteer services offer people of all types opportunities for wholesome, constructive use of leisure time. The opportunities for such activities are so extensive and the needs so great that everyone can find some service that fits his own peculiar interests and abilities if he only has an underlying desire to help his fellow men.

Examples of the many possibilities in volunteer services are summarized in this section. Some are very personal and deal with needs on a completely person-to-person basis apart from any organizational considerations. Others can be performed only within the framework of an organized program of social services. Some pertain to social action to reform undesirable conditions, while others involve welfare activities to alleviate the misery of persons who are the victims of those conditions. Volunteer services take many forms and are provided within a broad range of social contexts. The volunteer service bureau, family services agency, or county welfare office can help one find projects in his community which need volunteers.

1. *Needs of the family and home.* Adoption of dependent children usually performs a twofold service: it gives children a home, and it gives a home children. One of the greatest current needs in adoption is for families that will accept children of a racial background different from their own. This takes a special kind of parent. Few can meet the high qualifications demanded, for in a society filled with prejudice against minority groups extra problems are typically encountered in this kind of adoption. The high standards set by reputable adoption agencies are established to protect the child, the adoptive couple, and the child's natural parents or unmarried mother.

Several types of foster homes are needed in most communities. During the investigation and waiting period which precedes the adoption of an infant, it needs a home. Foster parents take care of the child, usually receiving reimbursement for the direct costs of such care from the agency that has supervision over the child.

Foster homes for delinquent children are used in conjunction with probation services. There they learn to live within the rules of society in an environment more conducive to their welfare than an institution would be. They are given moral support for the solution of personal problems and help in personal and social development that is lacking in their usual place of residence. Information about these programs and the need for them can be obtained through courts, probation officers, and correctional institutions of a community.

Foster homes for the aged are a recent but expanding development. Many elderly people are unable to meet all their needs alone, yet they are not handicapped so much that they need to be confined to a nursing home. Others are lonely. Foster home care provides such persons with living accommodations in a private home, meals, laundry, and the assurance that somebody will be available at night in case of emergency. The arrangements are similar to those of foster homes for children. The hostess is paid a modest fee, and special arrangements are made for medical care.

Homemaker services enable the ill, bereaved, and handicapped to remain in their own homes instead of going to hospitals, nursing homes, or other institutions. Trained, responsible homemakers also take care of a household when illness or disability of the mother threatens normal family life. They adapt to the individual needs of each family, doing all that is possible to help its members maintain a happy home environment. They prepare meals, supervise children, and take care of shopping and household affairs in general. Work with a given family may range from two to eight hours daily for as many as five days a week.

"Meals on Wheels" programs bring hot meals into the homes of partially handicapped people at regular intervals. This is another service needed by many elderly people, for they are not apt to receive a balanced diet without such help.

Day care for young children whose mothers work is another service provided by many churches. This program is especially important in the inner city, where widows, divorcees, unmarried mothers, and mothers in economically deprived families cannot both earn the necessities of life and at the same time care for their children during working hours.

Children from such families are often deprived of fathers through death or divorce and grow up without male companionship. Men can use their spare time to take such children to ball games, on fishing excursions, or into other activities, with or without children of their own, under programs like that of the recently organized "Fathers-at-Large."

2. *Services to the handicapped.* More than 5,000,000 people in the United States are mentally retarded. Three out of every hundred babies are mentally deficient. Nearly 200,000 patients live in public institutions for the mentally retarded. Others are in private hospitals. Some are in foster homes administered by licensed practical nurses or other specialists. Many are cared for by parents who feel disgraced and isolate themselves as well as the children.

Some of the institutionalized retarded are never visited by relatives or friends. Volunteers can give them cheer at birthdays and other special celebrations, visit them regularly, supply essential clothing and other items, and give picnics and other outings to promote their happiness. Social services, recreational opportunities, assistance to teachers, religious activities, letter-writing, story-reading, and help to staff members are examples of the kinds of help needed.

The blind and visually handicapped can benefit from the services of people who will read to them, write letters for them, and transcribe books and other printed material in Braille or on tape for their use.

Camping and recreational programs for crippled and other handicapped people, recreation and entertainment at parties and holidays, the collection and distribution of Christmas gifts for institutionalized persons, and assistance in programs of physical, recreational, and occupational therapy are other activities for which volunteers are needed.

3. *Problems of illness and health.* The "Candy-Striper" program of volunteer services by teen-agers and similar services by "Gray Ladies" and other adults in hospitals is receiving increased attention because of the significant work they accomplish for patients. Giving them fresh water, delivering mail, caring for flowers, running errands, assisting in business offices, supervising the information desk for visitors, writing letters, reading to patients, and even playing games with them are among the types of help given. Rolling bandages, shampooing hair, assisting in therapeutic swimming, leading musical therapy activities,

and helping the disabled redevelop physical skills are other activities provided by volunteers.

Comeback, Inc., is a national organization formed to work solely in the field of therapeutic recreation for disabled children, the chronically ill, the aged, and the handicapped. Other associations give guidance and help to people who suffer from such afflictions as mental retardation, polio, and heart disease.

Halfway houses are needed for emotionally disturbed, mentally ill, retarded, alcoholic, and other patients who are not yet well enough to be fully released from special care, yet not ill enough to warrant full hospital treatment. Volunteers can aid in providing the services necessary to make such programs truly rehabilitative.

For over sixteen years Shut-In Clubs, Inc., of Everett, Washington, has been giving free services to shut-ins in the community. "Volunteer friends" visit chronically ill patients on a regular basis. They show that someone cares for them as an individual and thus contribute much to the therapy of many hospitals.

Hobby advisors in rest homes, recreational leaders, and supervisors of group activities often play a significant part in the restoration of physical and mental health. Patients can be led to help other patients in many group activities.

Programs of medical research in hospitals and universities sometimes need volunteers. These volunteers serve either as controls by which to verify the effects of treatment administered to others or as patients who are the direct objects of experimentation. Behavioral scientists also need the cooperation of persons who will fill out questionnaires, cooperate in interviews, and provide other information dealing with their health in relationship to life experiences.

One of the most significant volunteer programs to promote physical health is the blood donor program of the Red Cross. If there is anyone who should be eager to give a pint of his own blood to help spare the life of someone else, it should be the person who believes that his salvation is provided through the shed blood of Jesus Christ. Fundamentalists ought to be in the front row of donors to this good cause!

4. *Victims of social problems.* In spite of specific biblical mandates to visit prisoners in the name of Christian mercy (Matt. 25:36, 39, 43, 44), relatively few services are offered to prisoners

171

by churches besides an occasional gospel team program, pastoral visit, or chaplaincy appointment. The example of Friendly Visitors, the Roman Catholic organization for visiting inmates in New York's House of Detention for Women, could be emulated in many communities. Their acts of kindness to the prisoners and assistance in finding them work upon release have led them to form plans for a halfway house where the women can readjust to freedom upon release.

In London a club has been formed under auspices of the Center-After-Care Association, which uses volunteer leadership to help the wives of men serving prison sentences. Left lonely and unsupported, such women need help of many kinds with problems of finances, domestic worries, and marital adjustment. The resulting group therapy may also have a significantly wholesome impact upon the readjustment of their husbands to society.

"Operation Teen-ager" in Georgia uses inmates of the state's Industrial Institute for Boys to speak before high-school audiences to explain how they got to prison. Their experiences give students insight into the detrimental nature of many of their own activities and presumably help to prevent juvenile delinquency. Dropouts Anonymous in Los Angeles uses techniques similar to Alcoholics Anonymous to encourage school dropouts to enter vocational training and thus indirectly to keep out of trouble.

Big Brothers of America and its twin, the Big Sister Association, need large numbers of qualified volunteers to work with boys and girls on an individual basis. Numerous community recreation centers and specialized programs of service clubs have similar needs as they work with youth to prevent future trouble or to rehabilitate those who already have slipped.

The needs of alcoholics and problem drinkers are so difficult to meet that few persons can help other than those who themselves have been rehabilitated. Alcoholics Anonymous and its related societies for family members, Alateens and Alanon, can receive significant assistance from Christians who themselves have suffered from the curse of alcoholism. The thirteen points stressed in AA's program are closely related to the Christian gospel.

Many large metropolitan areas have counseling services and other help available for persons who are contemplating suicide. The best known of these are the Samaritans in London and the Suicide Bureau in Los Angeles. At least one person is always available at a listed and advertised telephone number. Volunteers are available on call to go to the person in need if he will not come to the church or office out of which the service operates. Counseling to convince potential suicides that life is worth living is a service which has more direct opportunities for religious witnessing than most other forms of social service. Concerned evangelical Christians would perform a distinct service by co-operating across denominational lines to provide a suicide service in each major metropolitan area that does not yet have it.

Other opportunities relate to a wide variety of special needs. The victims of racial discrimination, slum dwellers, American Indians on reservations and in cities, migrant agricultural workers, refugees, prostitutes, and numerous others have needs that often can be met more effectively by lay volunteers than by professional church-hired workers. For people clustered in specific geographical areas, a Peace Corps type program during the summer vacations of high-school and college-age youth may be an appropriate way of providing special services like day camps, arts and crafts programs, repairing of buildings, erection of sanitary facilities, and remedial education work. Many indirect benefits of wholesome intergroup understanding and interpersonal relationships will also flow from such projects.

Old age, which basically is a blessing, has become a problem for many people because of the way the aged are treated. A large number of special services are needed for retired adults. Volunteer visiting can bring the older person back into contact with the world outside his residence, help him in the reading and writing of letters, give an outlet for expressing problems and draining off tensions, give help in small errands, cheer the despondent and sorrowing, advise about financial and other problems, and in various ways promote mental and spiritual health.

The Adopt-A-Grandparent Plan of B'nai B'rith Young Adults could be emulated by other groups. Youths give of themselves, their time, and their dedication to be companions of institutionalized older citizens on a standing and regular basis. The results benefit both the youth and the aged.

Telephone calls made daily to the home of an older person or couple is another valuable service provided at nominal cost by certain groups. They provide reassurance, companionship, entertainment, assistance in time of need, and security to the elderly or disabled and to their relatives. If there is no answer, some-one is sent immediately to discover what help is needed. The service can be furnished by persons who themselves are handi-capped, thus serving a double goal.

Social centers and clubs where the aged can secure companion-ship and recreation are provided by many churches and com-munity agencies. These often need qualified volunteers to direct the program, although much of the work can be done by the elderly themselves. Transportation help by volunteers for visits to the medical doctor, shopping, church, and other activities is often highly desirable for the elderly who are slightly disabled. Employment services for senior citizens capable of working, recreational therapy, meals on wheels, and numerous other ser-vices are provided for the aged with volunteer help in many com-munities.

5. *Economic needs.* In one respect all of the needs to which reference has been made are economic. In addition, however, there may be a place for programs designed specifically to help the economically deprived. Neighbors can no longer harvest the crops or cultivate the fields of the average disabled worker, but they can support welfare agencies that give relief. Often there is a delay between an application for aid and the granting of help. Church welfare committees and other groups can meet the interim needs if they have the authority to act immediately. People cannot quit eating while their application is being proc-essed. A central storeroom for contributed food and clothing might be an appropriate outlet for some material help by church-es and concerned people. Even contributed trading stamps may be used to purchase some needed supplies.

Gifts of repairable clothing, furniture, and housewares to the Salvation Army and Goodwill Industries serve a double purpose. They help disabled persons who get the work of collecting, re-pairing, and selling the items, and they help the underprivileged who cannot buy new goods.

An "Adopt a Poverty Child" plan to give children who are the victims of poverty help on a personal basis as a supplement to other welfare programs has been proposed by former Senator Keating of New York. A small sum of money and an encourag-ing letter would be sent monthly to the "adopted" child by the contributor. With proper qualifications and precautions, there are numerous other similar possibilities.

6. *Help to Foreigners.* Many overseas relief programs need volunteers to make quilts, roll bandages, pack medicines, ship clothing, collect and ship books, and the like. Refugees from Eastern Europe and the Middle East can be brought to a new home in the United States or Canada with the help of sponsors who will guarantee that their needs will be met during the period of adjustment. An International Executive Service Corps dedicated to supplying volunteer management consultants to private industries in underdeveloped nations has recently been formed.

The excellent work of the Peace Corps is well known, but not so well known is the fact that it will accept qualified volunteers of all ages, not youth alone. Many missionary organizations are securing volunteers for one- or two-year terms or even for a summer to work on the foreign field supporting professional missionaries in their daily tasks. The Rev. Robert N. Meyers proposed in the July 17, 1964, issue of *Christianity Today* that a Christian Service Corps be organized as an interdenominational lay movement with a specifically evangelistic purpose. It would use Christians for short terms in a wide range of skills usable in the church's missionary ventures.

Foreign visitors, especially students in colleges and universities, need to be shown friendship and hospitality (Heb. 13:2). Taking them into one's home regularly to participate in family recreation, cook a meal, and share in social life will be an enriching experience for the giver. It will contribute to a wholesome perspective toward our nation and a mind that is more open to the Christian gospel.

7. *Community services.* Every community provides many opportunities to work for its improvement. The vision of a need for urban renewal often comes from people outside of their occupational roles who basically serve as volunteers investigating the problem and developing interest. People displaced by urban renewal, especially Negroes, the aged, and the unemployed, may need special attention in finding substitute housing.

Welfare agencies and social action groups in every community need volunteers for activities like those referred to elsewhere in

175

this chapter and also for fund-raising. It is wise to investigate before cooperating, especially in the case of organizations whose direct ministry is not obvious in the community. Some charitable organizations do little besides paying the salaries of their administrators and printing public relations advertisements, fund appeals, and leaflets. This, of course, is true of so-called religious agencies as well. Many a dollar presumably given "in the name of Christ" has been siphoned off from God's work. It has gone into the hands of either deliberately corrupt confidence men operating a "front" or else to highly inefficient, badly administered programs which sound good on paper but achieve little in practice except "public relations."

8. *Educational problems.* Some educational ventures call for the services of part-time volunteers who assist the teachers. Facilities and supervisors for after-school-hours study are also greatly needed in many inner-city areas where people live in such crowded, noisy housing that school children have no opportunities to study at home. Membership on the school board and service on committees to study school dropouts and other current problems are usually unpaid tasks of volunteers elected or appointed to the position.

9. *Personal services.* Whenever volunteer services are given on a person-to-person basis, an element of friendliness is added to a program that otherwise might seem very bureaucratic and emotionally cold. The kindness of helping an institutionalized girl with a new hairdo, a hospitalized man with a shave or haircut, an illiterate adult with learning how to read, or an elderly person with housework may be either part of a formal program or a purely personal service offered by a kind friend. A Roman Catholic parish in Whittier, California, has organized the "Annettes." Dedicated to serving families in need of a helping hand during childbirth, illness, or death, these women provide food, help in the home, furnish transportation, babysit, take care of children, wash and iron clothes, and provide emergency night care.

Opportunities for deeds of kindness to other people are as great as the needs for them. The person who tries to be as sensitive to the needs of others as he is to his own needs will find that nearly everyone can use some form of his help. It may be only an encouraging word, a seemingly minor compliment, or a voice of cheer; or it may involve hours of sympathetic listening, recreational fellowship, or direct assistance with specific problems.

10. *Church activities.* The needs for volunteers in church work also are great. A large number and wide variety of volunteers can be used for assistance in church-related welfare projects, translating sermons into the sign language of the deaf, tape-recording services for playback to shut-ins, extension work to bring Sunday school to those who cannot attend, friendly visiting in the name of the church, community canvassing to seek prospects for church welfare services and for membership, sponsorship of servicemen's centers, projects for migrant laborers in the community, gospel teams to missions and weak churches, camping programs, renovation of church equipment, service projects for church members and friends who are away in the armed forces, programs of city missions, help in Christian community centers, office work in the church, and conventional programs of education, recreation, social activities, and spiritual ministries.

The establishment of weekly Bible study groups for friends and neighbors in one's home can be a very rewarding experience with great evangelistic opportunities. Informal coffee breaks with neighboring housewives and other social recreational activities present opportunities for friendship which also have evangelistic overtones.

The Roman Catholic Tape-of-the-Month Club was organized in 1959 to present "The Word of God and an explanation of liturgical action" through the personality of a dynamic church leader by tape recordings. No charge except return postage is made for the use of tapes, but they are sent only to those who promise to use them for two discussions every month. Protestants, especially in small, isolated churches, may have educational and inspirational needs that could be satisfied in a similar way.

One area of ministry often neglected by Protestants is the inner city. When slums have surrounded a church, it has typically moved to the suburbs. Its plea has been that the old location was no longer an effective field of evangelism, and people were moving away. Yet in fact the nearby population was increasing, not decreasing. The inner-city church that survives usually is deprived of capable leadership as well as of finances for its program at the very time when both are needed more than ever.

Prosperous churches would do well to appoint capable lay leaders on an annual basis to help weak and struggling churches with their educational and other ministries. Such appointments would give them the official blessing, recognition, and prayers of the home church.

Through a significant organization founded in 1958 to "put Christianity into overalls," Christians at home can help to serve missionaries and others overseas. The "Assistance Corps" program of DATA International enables persons who have knowledge and skills in a wide variety of trades and professions to give person-to-person solutions to practical problems submitted by missionaries, Peace Corps workers, and others who are helping to raise the level of living in underdeveloped nations. Its central office in Palo Alto, California, is staffed almost entirely with volunteers. The mechanical drawings, plans for home-built equipment, techniques for processing agricultural and forestry products, methods of irrigation, health measures, human relations techniques, and other suggestions are submitted on request by appropriate volunteers selected from the thousands on file. They represent nearly the entire scope of human knowledge and skills.

Skills Used in Volunteer Services

The needs for volunteer service activities are so great that a simple list of specific opportunities available in the typical metropolitan area or state would more than fill all the pages of this chapter. The needs can be summarized broadly according to problems, as in the preceding discussion, or they can be classified according to the types of skill demanded of those who contribute the services. The New Jersey Division on Aging, for instance, has compiled a list of "Service Activities for Your Leisure Time." It includes twelve types of skill:[2]

1. Care skills: Helping in the home of a neighbor; helping the handicapped person to eat; sitting with elderly people; sitting with patients at home; helping with self-care activities; sitting with children; caring for pets and plants.

2. Clerical skills: Addressing envelopes; acting as librarian; keeping records of service; filing; typing; sending birthday mes-

[2] Reprinted by permission of the Division, Trenton, N. J.

sages for groups; sorting magazines and reading materials; mimeographing.

3. Creative art skills: Making decorations for a party; framing pictures for an exhibit; designing scenery for a play; making posters; entertaining others; making favors for a party; taking a snapshot for a slide; setting up a display or exhibit; writing a news item; writing a book review; rearranging furniture in a room; planning a color scheme for a program; utilizing scrap materials for a project.

4. Educational skills: Showing slides or films of a trip; monitoring a test; coaching or refereeing a game; teaching a child to read or write; teaching a foreigner to speak English; teaching an American to speak a foreign language; helping a foreigner to pass a citizenship test; helping the underprivileged person to learn social habits; training volunteers to do a job; helping the handicapped with good grooming; reading to the partially sighted or blinded person; describing interesting experiences; talking to a group on a special subject; speaking over the radio or on TV; teaching someone to read music.

5. Handicraft skills: Helping to paint and repair facilities; building shelves and storage spaces; building outdoor facilities; making things for others; painting furniture.

6. Homemaking skills: Baking and cooking for a fair; serving refreshments; mending and sewing; serving meals; cleaning for a neighbor; preparing a hot meal for others; shopping for a neighbor; measuring a hem; planning a menu.

7. Leadership skills: Attending meetings as the representative of a group; acting as chairman of a committee; acting as a member of a board; being concerned about organization and people; planning and conducting a hobby show; supervising youth activities; recognizing the service of others; stimulating interest in projects; identifying worthwhile causes; demonstrating special skills; organizing groups for a purpose; conducting an information and referral service; planning and conducting trips; arranging the details of a program or exhibit; planning and conducting a fund drive; working as a council member.

8. Mechanical skills: Playing phonograph records for others;

179

rolling bandages; wrapping gifts and packages; packing kits for agencies; operating technical equipment; driving a car for others.

9. Physical skills: Providing messenger service; carrying supplies and equipment; pushing a wheelchair in a hospital; pushing a cart to the wards in a hospital; helping a neighbor move furniture or rugs; reaching to the top shelf for another person.

10. Participation skills: Attending school board meetings; participation in Inter-Faith Week; joining in Brotherhood Week; serving on committees and boards; meeting with senior citizens for a purpose; voting in local elections; joining and working in an organization; contributing financially in whatever way possible; submitting items for a hobby show.

11. Public relations skills: Promoting civic responsibility; acting as a receptionist; collecting money for a fund drive; making telephone calls to others; listening to others complain; presenting a positive viewpoint; selling at a bazaar or sale.

12. Social skills: Visiting the home-bound; welcoming newcomers; inviting friends in for tea; stimulating participation by others; showing an interest in the individual person; giving sincere praise; telling a good joke.

Qualifications for Volunteer Service

The qualifications for voluntary services vary with the tasks and social situations involved in each specific opportunity. Basic to all others, from the Christian perspective, is a sincere desire to love one's neighbor as he loves himself. Opening oneself to see others' needs is a primary prerequisite to helping them. Demonstrating love through action, not holding it merely as a vague, subjective feeling, is one of the ways by which love is increased. Like other virtues, love is learned by practicing love!

Some people can express love directly to other people in personal services; others are better qualified to furnish indirect services which do not involve face-to-face relationships. But all Christians should let their love be "without dissimulation" (Rom. 12:9); it should not be insincere.

Many of the people for whom social services are provided seem to be cynical, shrewd, and unappreciative when they are offered "tender loving care." Some of them have learned that donors of help sometimes have ulterior motives or seek personal recognition and other rewards for their efforts. Those whom they "help" have been used as instruments in a struggle for prestige, influence, or praise. When help is offered to those who have been victimized, they ask, "What's his racket?" or "What's in it for him?" or "What strings are attached?" They have seen so few instances of true love that they do not know experientially what it means. Not knowing what love is, they can hardly be expected to respond to vague verbal accounts of "the love of God."

Volunteers who work directly with the needy should be ready to accept them as they are. Help should not be given with an implicit price tag that insists upon rewards of compliance with the helper's demands, expressions of gratefulness to the helper, or conversion to the helper's religion. Such help is not *freely* given (see Matt. 10:8b). It is not a worthy example of the kind of love God bestows upon all men (Matt. 5:43-48).

That volunteer work which is done in the name of Christ must be reviewed to make certain it is well planned and carefully excuted so that it will fit the whole pattern of God's love in reconciling men to Himself. The feelings of those who receive help will hence be given careful attention as well as the feelings of those who provide it. The donor's personal maturity, ability to accept differences between people, lack of a driving desire to turn other people into images of himself, respect for even the most despised of mankind as persons created in the image of God and as people for whom Christ died, sacrificial kindness even when rebuffed, and warmth of loving acceptance will kindle a responsive chord in the recipients even if a wholesome response is not evident immediately.

Willingness to take leisure from oneself in order to *see* the needs of others will be followed by a willingness to use leisure time to *help meet* the needs of others. Vision precedes action, but action helps vision to grow.

Effects of Volunteer Services

Obviously the most important result of services contributed to meet human needs is that people are helped with their problems. Friendliness is therapeutic; it helps to heal physical and mental ills. There are other important effects as well, however.

When such work is done with the specific blessing of a church or under its auspices, community leaders and agencies become favorably disposed toward Christians. They will listen more readily when the church speaks on other matters. This will enable the church to become more truly the "conscience of the community." Some persons also will open their minds to serious consideration of the gospel, so the evangelistic ministry of the church will indirectly benefit. The quietly spoken word of a Christian in relatively casual contacts with others does more for evangelism than most sermons and "official" church publicity. (See Prov. 15:23; 25:11; I Pet. 3:15.)

Some Americans carry in their minds the puritan perspective that recreation is sin. They have a burden of guilt for the way in which they use their leisure time. This burden obviously can be removed by using such time in volunteer services which help others.

Time is a heavy burden for many people who are retired, unemployed, or working only forty of the 168 hours in a week. Their boredom can be relieved and they can find meaning in life by engaging in worthwhile volunteer services. The satisfactions of being useful, knowing one has carried out a task well, recognizing and using one's own particular abilities, and working constructively with other people make this one of the most recreating forms of recreational behavior.

Self-fulfillment results from the adventures involved in even the most monotonous service, the change of pace from workaday life, self-expression, a sense of accomplishment, identification with others who are either needy or fellow workers helping to meet needs, and the satisfaction of knowing one is doing his part to counteract problems and crises in the surrounding world. Self-interest is thus intricately related to interest in others. One cannot love his neighbor as himself unless he loves himself!

Whatever men possess in the way of property, skills, and the graces of love, joy, and peace is enhanced by sharing with others. The more one gives of himself, the more love and happiness he has to enrich the lives of himself and others. "Give, and it shall be given unto you; good measure, pressed down, and shaken together, and running over, shall men give into your bosom. For with the same measure that ye mete withal it shall be measured to you again" (Luke 6:38).

Church Involvement in Volunteer Services

Every organized group within the church ideally ought to have a service project. Service to others in group activities will teach the significant lesson that the church is an instrument of service, not an institution to be served. Too many youth groups today expect to be waited on hand and foot; they see themselves as to be served and do not realize that instead they ought to serve. This misconception often begins in the early formative years of religious education and snowballs along to the detriment of the church, the persons in it, and thus the total work of Christ. Even small children in a Sunday school class can brighten the lives of the residents of a nearby nursing home, institution for the mentally retarded, retirement apartment, or mental hospital by singing their praises to God, contributing handiwork to the patients, and bringing their cheer on a quarterly or monthly basis.

The coordination and administration of church-sponsored volunteer services should be a major task of the committee on Christian social concern recommended in Chapter 5. It also should stimulate members to participate in volunteer service activities of community agencies outside the church. This will help to bring the gospel into all areas of social life. It will help the church serve its function as the light, salt, and quickening conscience of society.

When the church forthrightly gives its blessing to volunteer services in worthy community agencies, the sense of guilt of some Christians who now are active in such ministries will be removed. They will no longer see these agencies as competitors of the church. They will recognize more clearly that their work in the community is as much an aspect of Christian service as making table decorations for a church banquet, attending an inspirational rally, or planning a church social. They will be reminded of the need for faithfulness in their Christian witness and be strengthened for it.

The committee on Christian social concern can lead the church in discovering unmet needs which church organizations or members can help to fill. It can make the initial contacts with program leaders and agency administrators who need volunteer help. It can recruit qualified members for participating in volunteer services. The Holy Spirit will stimulate the minds of all who conscientiously seek out community needs and sincerely ask God how Christians ought to help meet them.

The administrative work of such activities should not fall on the shoulders of the pastor. He already has more than enough work! This is a task for laymen. Certain laymen retired from their regular work or with leisure time to donate can be used as volunteers or part-time employees to administer business affairs or supervise volunteer services.

The church ought to remember in its prayers the daily vocational influence of its members and their volunteer services to community agencies and people in need as well as the foreign missionaries, local church programs, and problems like illness which conventionally receive the bulk of attention. Often it is appropriate for a church to pay the incidental expenses of its volunteers. Then none will be prevented from serving by his own economic problems, and official recognition is given to those who serve. Members then will be reminded that they are engaged in "full-time Christian service." They will work more alertly and consistently for the glory of God. No one can be a Christian on only a part-time basis.

Problems in Volunteer Services

In addition to the routine problems of organizing, administering, and coordinating any program of activities, certain special difficulties should also be mentioned.

First, church people have a tendency to feel that their responsibility has been met when they have merely discussed a problem, perhaps in a committee. Talk may relieve the emotions of the speaker, but there is a great gap between stating an ideal and implementing it. We must become "doers of the word, not hearers only, deceiving ourselves" (Jas. 1:22).

Second, when it is recognized that certain types of people will benefit by their participating in a volunteer program, there is a temptation to make work for them. But volunteer work should be valuable in its own right; it should be *real work*, not just *made work*. Youth, the physically handicapped, and others will soon lose all their enthusiasm and thus all the benefit of volunteer services if they are given only meaningless tasks. This implies that the significance of the work should be made clear to the volunteers, lest they fail to see it.

Third, volunteers usually need an orientation to their task, sometimes even relatively lengthy training. Every successful program includes sound recruitment procedures, recognition of the interests and capabilities of the volunteers, suitable placement and use of the workers, democratic operation of the program so that the volunteers are not treated as if they were inferior beings, and recognition for services performed.

Fourth, an unhealthy professionalism is sometimes found among medical personnel, recreational leaders, educators, and social workers. They may prefer not to have volunteer help with a program lest it be revealed that many of their duties do not require professional training. Nevertheless, professional people are in a better position to appreciate the work of volunteers than are outsiders. The best proof of the need for volunteers and of the fact that they will not displace the professions lies in demonstration programs which have successfully coordinated professional and volunteer workers.

Fifth, volunteers must recognize their limitations and not try to usurp the place of professional people. Job analysis is greatly needed in the helping professions to indicate how to use the time of professional workers more effectively. Many of their routine duties can be assigned to volunteers, leaving them more time for the tasks which demand professional skills and insight.

Sixth, the aim in all volunteer services should be to rehabilitate people with problems rather than solely to meet immediate short-term needs. Identification with them by personal involvement is akin to the Incarnation, when God identified Himself with mankind in the person of Jesus Christ. When the word becomes deed, as the Word became flesh, the Christian gospel will become clearer to the world.

The Challenge of Volunteer Service

Every community is bursting with problems that could be alleviated by widespread Christian involvement. The joy of helping to conquer ignorance, poverty, suffering, and disease is not restricted to missionaries and members of the Peace Corps who go to distant underdeveloped countries! It is available to all who voluntarily shoulder the burden and, carrying their cross, follow the Servant of man.

If they are not blinded by pride or prejudice, Christians who look out over the multitudes in their own community will discern many needs that can be filled only if volunteers supplement the services of professional people in public, private, and church-related institutions and programs. Personal applications of Christian love are greatly needed to enrich institutional programs and agency services.

SUGGESTIONS FOR DISCUSSION AND STUDY

1. Large-scale organization of social welfare is increasingly necessary in a large-scale society in which no community, no state, and no region is self-sufficient. How can the values of direct personal involvement and friendly face-to-face help be preserved in large welfare programs? What role should the church play in this?

2. Since contributions to the Red Cross blood bank may be used by nonchristians who indulge in activities displeasing to God, is it right for a Christian to donate his blood to it? Is he helping to promote "the works of darkness" when he does so? How can the example of Jesus Christ help to resolve this problem? Was His blood shed only for those who are worthy? (See Bible passages like John 13:34; Rom. 5:6-10; and I John 2:2.)

3. To what extent are the members of your church unconcerned about the social needs of people in their neighborhood, in the larger community, and at their place of daily activity? Why do many lack a social concern? Would a program of volunteer services sponsored by your church awaken their Christian compassion? How do they differ from members who have a vital social concern?

4. Survey the Bible to find examples of volunteer services. Which seem to be praised the most? Are any condemned? What are the practical implications of these Bible accounts for us today?

5. Have you ever observed instances of what apparently are ulterior motives in volunteer services of the church or community agencies? What were their effects? Did these volunteers do

good in spite of their imperfect motivations? Should the church do anything about this problem?

6. Compile a list of "right-wing" arguments against public welfare programs and in favor of voluntary welfare as a replacement for them. Then compile a list of "left-wing" arguments in favor of public welfare programs, holding that voluntary welfare cannot replace public services satisfactorily but can only supplement them. Evaluate the arguments in both lists. Try to discern the hidden assumptions and unexpressed motivations which are at the foundation of each as well as the direct statements. Which of the perspectives on each side of this controversy seem close to New Testament principles, and which seem opposed to them? Which seem the most realistic for the kind of world in which we live? (If you are a scholar, a comparison of the social gospel movement and social Darwinism will richly supplement this study.)

7. Study social service agencies in your community to determine the uses they make of volunteers. What needs do volunteers meet? What skills must they have? What are their other qualifications? Where are the greatest needs for additional volunteers? Can you help to recruit them? How?

8. Interview one or more persons who provide foster home care or other volunteer services and several who receive them. What satisfactions does each receive? What special problems does each face?

9. Investigate the service projects of the American Friends Service Committee. (The central office is at 160 North 15th St., Philadelphia 2, Pa.) What do they accomplish for the recipients of their services? What rewards do the volunteers receive? Does their work suggest similar possibilities for your own denomination?

10. Keep a record of your use of time every day one full week. Use categories like work, sleep, eating, personal care (dressing, bathing, shaving, care of the hair, etc.), recreational reading, reading related to work, watching television, household duties, church attendance, church work, transportation to and from work, recreational social experiences, and volunteer services on behalf of others. Does your record represent good stewardship of your time?

187

RECOMMENDED READING

Action Course Volunteer Program. Washington, D. C.: Chamber of Commerce of the United States, Public Affairs Dept., 1963. A booklet describing an educational program to stimulate grass-roots activity in the political party of one's choice.

Bowser, Hallowell, "Bats in the Guava Trees," *Saturday Review,* Vol. 45, No. 51, (Dec. 29, 1962), 26. A description of DATA International and its origin, work, and types of problems solved with volunteers.

Cohen, Nathan E., editor, *The Citizen Volunteer.* New York: Harper and Brothers, 1960. A symposium of 19 chapters on the responsibility, motives, role, and opportunities of volunteers in modern society.

Council of National Organizations for Adult Education, *Probing Volunteer-Staff Relations.* New York: Association Press, 1963. A kit for the self-inventory of voluntary organizations.

Grimes, Howard, *The Rebirth of the Laity.* New York: Abingdon Press, 1962. The biblical basis, historical background, meaning, service, and renewal of the lay members of the Body of Christ.

A Handbook for Volunteers in the Field of Aging. Topeka, Kansas: Kansas State Dept. of Social Welfare, Div. of Services for the Aging, 1960. An excellent description of how communities can provide necessary services for the aging, especially in nursing homes, through the coordination of volunteers; many specific activities and resources are described.

Public Health Services Division, Community Health Services, *Directory of Homemaker Services,* 1963. Washington, D. C.: U. S. Dept. of Health, Education, and Welfare, 1964. A list of 303 agencies with homemaker services and descriptions of the kinds of families receiving services, fees charged, policies, etc.

PART V:

EVALUATING CHRISTIAN SOCIAL CONCERN

Chapter 10

Measuring Success

For other foundation can no man lay than that is laid, which is Jesus Christ.

Now if any man build upon this foundation gold, silver, precious stones, wood, hay, stubble;

Every man's work shall be made manifest: for the day shall declare it, because it shall be revealed by fire; and the fire shall try every man's work of what sort it is.

If any man's work abide which he hath built thereupon, he shall receive a reward.

If any man's work shall be burned, he shall suffer loss: but he himself shall be saved; yet so as by fire (I Cor. 3:11-15).

GOD IS THE ULTIMATE JUDGE OF THE SUCCESS OR FAILURE OF ANY and all programs of social concern. Christians are warned in the Scriptures not to set themselves up as judges over others (Matt. 7:1-5; Luke 6:37-42; Rom. 2:1; 14:10-13; Jas. 4:11-12; etc.). At the same time, however, they are told to judge their own activities and evaluate the programs they participate in to make sure that they are pleasing to God (II Cor. 13:5; Gal. 6:4; I Thess. 5:21-22; I John 4:1-3). This certainly applies to group activities as well as to those of individuals. Churches are admonished to listen to the Holy Spirit's judgment (Rev. 2:1-3:22), and even "nations" are accountable to God (Matt. 25:31-46).

The opinion that the results of Christian work should be left entirely to the judgment of God has hindered a great deal of service done in His name. It has been used as an excuse for carelessness, sloppiness, and ineffectiveness in Christian service.

191

Occasionally it is used as a cloak for sins of omission, goal displacement, or even crimes like misappropriation of funds.

Everyone who is involved in systematic activity tends to evaluate it subconsciously and intuitively, if not consciously and objectively. The conclusion that one church has "an active program" and another "is dead," for instance, is the product of evaluation. Yet the very people who pass such judgments may inconsistently oppose a research effort to evaluate the effectiveness of church-related programs. In their claim that faithfulness is the only important consideration, they forget that one can faithfully pursue unchristian goals. It is possible to overlook major matters by faithful attention to minor details (see Matt. 23:23-24). The total situation within which duties are faithfully performed is just as relevant as the faithfulness of performance.

Standards of Success

The only realistic test of a program relates to its goals. If the goals have been met, the program is a success; if they have not, it is a failure. Hence all that has been said in previous chapters about the biblical foundation for Christian social concern, society's need, and means of implementing social responsibility is relevant to evaluative research.

Evaluative research should examine what has been done to promote the work and the will of God in society as a whole, in the local community, and in the church as an institution. The effects of the programs on all those levels, both on persons who participate in them and on those who received the social services, are especially important.

There may be signs of great success on certain of these levels but only of failure on others. A sick person who has received medical treatment may still be sick, but not as sick as he would have been without the help. Similarly, the poor may still be poor, the schizophrenic may still be mentally ill, and others who received help may still be needy. This by itself does not prove that no good has been accomplished.

Goals must not be confused, however. When a person needs an appendectomy, his primary concern is with the effectiveness of the doctor and hospital for surgical operations, not with whether they promote the religious objectives of his church. Indeed, he would probably reject the services of a Christian doctor who is known to be a poor surgeon. Similarly with programs of social service. The test of their effectiveness, all other things being equal, is their performance in providing the services.

A social welfare agency is not a church; a church is not a social welfare agency. Social work is social work, not a disguise for conventional preaching of the gospel. The criteria for measuring success must be consistent with the primary goals of the program being evaluated.

We live in a society which tends to evaluate everything in materialistic terms. Neither numbers nor dollars are the most important criteria of success. Doing good in the name of Christ brings its own reward. A kind act is a good act (see Matt. 10:42; 25:40; Heb. 13:16; etc.) even if it fails to win converts to Jesus Christ.

It is important to consider the indirect as well as the direct effects of our action. Achieving one desirable social change may set forces into motion that produce three or four undesirable ones. These latent consequences should be evaluated as well as those that are obvious. It is not easy to find them, but their long-range effects often have utmost significance.

What to Study

The general sketch of topics given below cuts across a wide variety of social welfare and social action programs. It is also useful, with suitable adaptations, for evaluating other church and community activities.

The first step is to specify the goals or objectives of the program. What are its purposes as seen by the board or committee behind the program, its administrators, professional workers, volunteers, recipients of services, sponsors or contributors, and interested friends and professional people in the community? Each can be asked to complete the statement, "The main purpose of . . . . . [this program] is . . . . . ," in twenty-five words or less. Do they all agree? If not, why not? Are the goals realistic? Frank, open discussion by all who are directly concerned and compiling a written record of agreements and disagreements can help to unify the group that is concerned with the project or at least explain the existing lack of unity.

This may lead to a study of the interests and needs the program is designed to meet. Exploratory fact-finding through interviews, questionnaires, group discussions, statistical analyses, and the like can help to discover existing problems. The workers, clients, and other interested or involved persons may identify different aspects of the problem or even see totally divergent needs for action.

Findings about needs in the community, especially if they extend beyond the needs for which a specific program is designed, may lead to a revision of goals. Long-term goals, intermediate goals which may be necessary to attain them, and specific practices which have immediate objectives should be coordinated so that none are at cross purposes with each other.

Study of the extent to which the goals of a program are actually being attained is not easy. It includes identifying observable criteria by which to test accomplishments.

The asking of relevant questions is often the chief key to successful research. Through such questions the problem of evaluation is broken into relevant component parts. It is often wise to add "else questions" to any study: what else, where else, how else, when else, who else, and why else. Such probing can help to reveal some of the indirect effects of the program.

Questions about achievement should be answered objectively as far as possible. Yet there will always be qualitative considerations in Christian service that will not lend themselves to objectification. Judgments must be made. Deliberation and examination of every possible contrary interpretation should enter into this process.

Evaluation should not overlook the methods and procedures used in a program. One set of possible administrative devices may be much less costly in time, personnel, and money than another and yet may achieve as good or better results. Opposing as well as supporting evidence for prevailing approaches should be examined. New methods should be sought and employed; after an initial period of adjustment they may turn out to be far more effective than the old.

The people engaged in a program deserve attention. Some are in a position to influence the flow of ideas. These "communication gatekeepers" may lend their prestige and support to innovations, or they may discourage them by deprecation. They may distort an idea deliberately or unwittingly, because they oppose it or fail to understand it. The study of personnel is a delicate aspect of research; it must be done with the greatest of tact and wisdom. Otherwise it may boomerang to the detriment of the entire program and its sponsoring institution.

It is often wise to attempt to determine what conditions would be if the program had never been established or if it were now discontinued. Many an agency which has outlived its usefulness continues primarily because entrenched bureaucrats have vested interests in it. This, obviously, is poor stewardship which requires prompt correction.

Evaluations should be based upon facts as much as possible, so when opinions are submitted, they should be sorted according to the pertinent qualifications of their sources. Even an atheist's critical look at Christianity can stimulate Christians to act more consistently according to their own principles. Agnostics and skeptics are hardly the ones, however, to interpret the Bible for the church!

To summarize, some of the chief considerations in testing the achievement of goals in social welfare and social action programs are questions about short-term and long-range purposes (*Why* are you conducting this program?), services provided (*What* are you doing?), leadership and staff (*Who implements* your services?), clients served (*For whom* are you doing it?), methods used (*How* are you serving them?), sanction (*With what authority* are you acting?), legitimation or sponsorship (*Who supports* your work?), cooperative working relationships (*Who cooperates* with you?), alternative avenues of service (*Who else* provides the same services? *Who competes* with you?), and, cutting across all else, effectiveness (*What effects* — direct and indirect — flow from your program?).

Planning

Careful evaluation inevitably will lead to careful planning for the future ministry of the agency or program studied. The planning process will be concerned with both an over-all strategy and the specific tactics or techniques to achieve that strategy. Planning is a process, not a fiat act.

Planning begins when someone sees a need, perhaps as a result of evaluative research which makes him dissatisfied with present achievements. Having a vision of how that need might be met or recognizing that a problem needs attention, he initiates discussion and study by interested people.

Definition of the problem and survey of existing conditions is followed by a process of policy determination. Various diagnoses are made as facts are related to the values and ideals of persons with diverse backgrounds and interests. Discussion of ends (goals, objectives, purposes) and means (methods, techniques, and programs to promote those ends) occurs.

This is accompanied by a process of legitimation in which interest groups often are at war with one another. Each tends to give its own prediction of what will occur in the future if various possible alternatives of action are pursued. If there is an underlying ideology or philosophy to which these interest groups all appeal, a consensus of opinion, or at least a majority interpretation and application, emerges. This becomes the basis for establishing a policy of action.

This policy is then elaborated into a specific program of action, and the program is implemented. During administration of the program, the feedback of information from those involved in it leads to modifications, review, and adjustments. Evaluation of successes and failures in turn leads back to the beginning of the cycle. Initiation, policy determination, legitimation, implementation, and evaluation are thus repeated, each cycle bringing new modifications.

In a changing world, the planning process is endless. If the world ends, men's programs also come to an end. Only as they remain living organisms ceaselessly adjusting to changes in their environment will social service agencies survive and continue to contribute to human welfare. The exceptions are not exceptions at all. Their planning takes place informally, casually, or on a personal level by some administrator. It is planning nevertheless.

Problems in Research

Many mistakes are made when programs are analyzed by novices in social research. It is therefore advisable, whenever possible, to secure the counsel of persons who have had specialized training in sociology, educational surveys, religious research, or other behavioral sciences. Many denominations have an office devoted to helping their congregations and boards with research problems. For a fee the services of commercial marketing research firms can be secured; these vary greatly in their competence to analyze religious and welfare agencies, so great care should be taken before making a contract with them.

Some common errors in research deserve attention here. When it is impossible to avoid these errors directly, the research findings should be qualified appropriately.

1. Check and cross-check the accuracy of analysis at every stage of the study. Everyone makes mistakes.

2. Whenever possible, a "control group" (persons not in the program studied but similar to those who are) should be observed as well as the "experimental group" of persons who have been in the program under investigation. Changes which may have occurred entirely apart from the program should not be attributed to it.

3. The logic leading to each conclusion should be analyzed carefully. Do the conclusions really follow from the evidence? What alternative conclusions are possible?

4. The statistical techniques used deserve careful scrutiny. Are they the most appropriate measures? Has allowance been made for chance variations such as sampling errors in extending findings to a larger universe? Minor variations should not be played up. Accuracy is important, but a specious accuracy gained by carrying out a computation to several decimal points is no more dependable than the original figures from which the statistics came.

5. Check on the reliability of all instruments used to collect and interpret data. Do the same results always occur from measuring the same phenomena by the same instrument? Repetition of observation, two or more forms of the instrument, and comparing half of the measurements with the other half are the chief techniques of checking reliability.

6. Check on the validity of instruments and questions used. Do they *really* indicate or measure what they purport to indicate? Logical analysis, the opinions of experts on the subject of study, comparisons with other instruments and questions dealing with the same or a related topic, and the analysis of groups who have an established position on the subject are techniques used to test validity.

197

7. If only a portion of persons in a program can be studied, take special care in selecting the sample of respondents. Usually they should be selected randomly, with every one having an equal chance of being included in the study. Their characteristics should be carefully compared with those of all persons in the total program to determine how representative they are, the ways in which they differ from the total group, and thus the extent to which conclusions based on them can be expected to represent the entire program.

8. Some persons included in the sample selected may not be available for study. How this biases the results should receive careful attention. Were they all away on a church retreat? Are they persons who refused to cooperate? Or what? How do they differ from those who were studied?

9. Concepts used in the study should be clearly defined. Most words have several possible meanings, so great care should be extended to everyone involved to make clear which meaning of every significant term is intended.

10. Questions should not be ambiguous. They should not imply two or more possible meanings, evoke divided responses from the same respondent, or create confusion in other ways. If a convert to Christianity is asked, "Did you stop beating your wife when you were converted?" he is condemned by either an affirmative or negative answer! Anticipate the reactions of all types of respondents. Use the guidance of many informed people in framing questions.

11. Report non-response and "don't know" answers to questions as well as those which are clearly answered in the prescribed manner. These sometimes are major indicators of special problems. Public opinion pollsters discovered this fact when they mistakenly predicted in 1948 that Thomas Dewey would become President of the United States. The votes of uncommitted respondents were not distributed in the same way as those of persons who expressed an opinion in pre-election surveys.

12. Allow for special problems in the interviewing or questionnaire situation. If rapport (a comfortable, unconstrained relationship of mutual confidence) is not established with the researcher, only "half-truths" may be given. These may be very

misleading. The vagaries and errors of memory must also be guarded against. People do not recall everything with an equal degree of accuracy!

Common sense in the research process will help to overcome many of these potential errors.

It is advisable to use a large number of advisors in planning research projects and in interpreting the data which they produce. "Without counsel purposes are disappointed: but in the multitude of counsellors they are established" (Prov. 15:22). The past experiences and educational background of people with diverse interests greatly enrich the research process and results.

Accuracy and care in methodological procedure should be a primary goal of Christians in their evaluative research. Biased findings and conclusions are lies. Followers of Him who is the Truth (John 14:6) should be led by the Spirit of Truth (John 14:17). They should not use their biased preconceptions as an excuse for accepting sloppy techniques that put them under the jurisdiction of the father of lies (John 8:44; see Eph. 4:25; Rev. 21:27; 22:15). The achievements of a program are seldom identical with its intentions. Dreams often differ from reality.

Errors of Evaluation

Another set of problems in evaluative research centers around certain temptations linked with "the lust of the flesh, the lust of the eyes, and the pride of life" (I John 2:15-17).

When a group which has neglected social responsibilities awakens to the call of God to love their neighbors, they may observe others who have church-sponsored welfare agencies and assume that their example should be precisely imitated. Such programs are established for the sake of keeping up with the "ecclesiastical Joneses" more than for the sake of meeting human needs. An agency can be obsolete the day it is opened, for the needs of 1870, 1900, or 1930 when the competing denomination's agencies were founded are different from the needs of today. If a need is already being met, even if not completely satisfactorily, it may be advisable to initiate new programs in other areas which are neglected completely, or nearly so, by other groups.

Looking ahead to anticipate forthcoming needs five, ten, and twenty years hence is highly appropriate in planning new programs and modifying old ones. Just as children are educated today for their lives in future years, agencies and programs should be planned today in pioneering ventures to help meet anticipated as well as present needs. Programs of social welfare erected just to show that we are "as good as" Catholics, Jews, or some Protestant groups do not rest upon high motives of Christian social concern. Pride is strongly condemned in the Scriptures.

Organizational leaders are subject to many diseases of bureaucracies. One of these is especially evident in evaluative research. The number of hours spent, dollars expended, records kept, committees attended, rallies held, or even clients contacted is a proper area of investigation, but such bookkeeping details do not indicate how *effective* the work has been. Independent measures of success or failure are necessary in order to get an accurate picture of effectiveness.

The belief that "Christ is the answer" has long been the basis for blinking eyes at human problems and pretending that Christians have none. This book has constantly intimated that Christ, in the broad sense of motivation, action, and guidance, is the answer. But it is not true that all problems are simply solved by narrowly conceived programs of evangelism.

The decision to receive Christ as Saviour and Lord is a first step in Christian living, but it must be followed by spiritual growth. It does not emancipate anyone from society, so it does not solve the common human needs that grow out of life in society. It gives a new perspective on life which is of great value, but it does not by itself give an unemployed worker new skills which are employable, a crippled man strength of body, nor a mentally retarded person the ability to read, write, and cope with life independently.

The expression "Christ is the answer" is used far too often as an excuse for inaction, a form of washing one's hands of God-given social responsibility. It reflects a pharisaical pride when it falsely implies that those who accept social responsibility are by virtue of that fact untrue to the gospel of salvation through faith in Jesus Christ.

That excuse is often linked with the belief that Christ's second coming is nigh. When He returns, all social problems will be solved. It is implied that hence the only responsibility of Christians is soul-winning. Persons who accept this view fail to recognize that throughout Christian history there have been people who momentarily expected Christ's return. No man knows the day and the hour. Waiting for and "hasting unto the coming" are implemented scripturally by godliness, holy conduct, purity of life, and obedience to the will of God (II Pet. 3:11-14; I John 3:2-3; I Thess. 5:1-11; I Pet. 1:13-16; etc.). Obedience necessitates both shouldering social responsibility and proclaiming the gospel to individuals.

Appeals to God's will should be made cautiously. The general outlines of this divine will are set forth clearly in the Bible, but the specific details are subject to human interpretation. If the Holy Spirit is truly leading a group, His will for the group will become evident to most of its members. It will not be revealed to one person alone. He who says dogmatically, "I know it is God's will for us to establish a child adoption agency," may be misled by an unrecognized desire for power. He who says, "God has revealed His will to me by a dream; we must purchase that property," may be the victim of psychological problems.

As in the missionary call of Barnabas and Paul, the Holy Spirit will speak to all who faithfully worship God (Acts 13:1-3), not just to one or two. During the exploratory stages of new projects it is therefore wise to refrain from using "God's will" as a club to beat others into submission to a specific program. Until the search for His will is satisfactorily concluded, men cannot be certain that they have attained it.

But this does not necessarily mean that if a project failed, it was not God's will. Sometimes God permits His children to experience failure. Something greater and better than they anticipated may result. They can learn from the experience and in turn teach others. The analysis and reporting of failures in Christian social welfare and social action hence may be even more important than the analysis and reporting of success.

Conclusion

Continual evaluation is necessary in all areas of Christian service. The planning process can never be final until the day when "the kingdoms of this world are become the kingdoms of our

201

Lord, and of his Christ; and he shall reign for ever and ever" (Rev. 11:15).

Evaluating the present status of a local church or denomination may make it recognize that it has fallen short of its social responsibilities to influence legislation and to help meet various welfare needs. It may reveal weaknesses in present programs that ought to be overcome as well as strengths that should be retained. It may also lead to pioneering programs of a kind previously unknown. Insights from Christian theology, ethics, sociology, psychology, political science, and other disciplines should be drawn together by evangelicals in a sincere desire that the will of God be done on earth as it is in heaven.

Christian influence on society is an effect of lives transformed by God's grace. It is evident in collective activities as well as in individual conduct. It results from demonstrating love to God by loving one's neighbor as oneself.

The ultimate test of Christian social responsibility will come on the great day when the King of kings says to the faithful,

> Come, ye blessed of my Father, inherit the kingdom prepared for you from the foundation of the world: For I was an hungred, and ye gave me meat: I was thirsty, and ye gave me drink: I was a stranger, and ye took me in: Naked, and ye clothed me: I was sick, and ye visited me: I was in prison, and ye came unto me. . . . Inasmuch as ye have done it unto one of the least of these my brethren, ye have done it unto me (Matt. 25:34-36, 40).

SUGGESTIONS FOR DISCUSSION AND STUDY

1. Why was God displeased with King David when he took a census of Israel (I Chron. 21:1-8)? Does this imply that God is displeased with church statistics? (See also Acts 1:15; 2:41; etc.) Do men violate God's will when they conduct research on the church and its programs?

2. List and evaluate the arguments for church planning and those used against it. How are planning and freedom interrelated? How does planning hinder freedom? How does it promote it?

3. Is it possible to identify various levels of success and failure in the area of Christian social responsibility? Consider immediate

and long-range results, temporal and eternal effects, influence on individuals, the church and the community, and similar consequences. What level has been reached by your church? By you?

4. What are some of the excuses, rationalizations, and other techniques used by Christians for not accepting adverse criticisms revealed by research? How valid is each? How can church leaders and agencies best cope with this problem when their own programs need improvement?

5. Can love be measured? How? How can the findings of your yardstick of love be applied?

6. Is the number of converts won through the direct influence of a church-sponsored welfare program a valid measure of its success? Is it ever a relevant criterion? Ought this to be the sole indicator of effectiveness? Why or why not?

7. How many and what percentage of your church's members live within walking distance of the church building? What proportion of all people within walking distance are members of your church? How many of them are unchurched? What are their characteristics? What problems are evident among them? What is your church doing to meet their spiritual and other needs?

8. Why has religious research emerged recently as a specialized profession? In which of its boards or commissions (Home Missions, Christian Education, Foreign Missions, etc.) does your denomination employ religious researchers? What are their qualifications, duties, and accomplishments?

9. Conduct a survey of representative people in your church and others in your community to discover how they feel about giving direct personal aid to needy persons on a voluntary basis, in comparison to paying taxes to support public programs of social welfare. Do your findings suggest any problems or attitudes to which your church ought to give attention?

10. Compile a list of research projects which have been conducted in your community. (Local colleges, city and county planning offices, public and private social service agencies, churches, businessmen's associations, service clubs, and the local library

are possible sources.) Compare the findings of these studies on topics related to social concern. If the conclusions disagree, are differences due to variations in the techniques of study, contrasting assumptions in the minds of the analysts, or other causes?

RECOMMENDED READING

Barzun, Jacques, and Graff, Henry F., *The Modern Researcher*. New York: Harcourt, Brace, 1957. An interesting discussion and description of basic principles of research and the writing of research reports, emphasizing subjects related to history.

Church Strategy Program, *A Look Inside Your Church and Community*. Valley Forge, Pa.: The American Baptist Home Missions Societies, Division of Church Missions, 1963. A manual for use in the self-study of churches and their communities.

Huff, Darrell, *How to Lie with Statistics*. New York: W. W. Norton and Co., rev. ed., 1954. A popular description of deceptive errors commonly made with statistics and how to avoid them.

Norton, Perry L., editor, *Search*. New York: National Council of the Churches of Christ in the U. S. A., 1960. The report of a national consultation on personnel needs in church planning and research; includes many practical suggestions for research and planning.

Spaulding, Helen F., editor, *Evaluation and Christian Education*. New York: National Council of the Churches of Christ in the U. S. A., 1960. Papers presented at the 1959 Conference on Evaluation in Christian Education; discussions of theological, educational, and practical issues in religious education research.

Young, Pauline V., and Schmid, Calvin F., *Scientific Social Surveys and Research*. Englewood Cliffs, N. J.: Prentice-Hall, third ed., 1956. An introduction to research which emphasizes the background, content, methods, principles, and analysis of social studies.

Index of Scripture References

(Paraphrases, allusions, etc. which are not accompanied by a specific reference in the text are omitted from this index. In some instances, to conserve space and avoid confusion, text references to single verses are included with references to longer passages of which the verses are a part.)

INDEX OF SCRIPTURE REFERENCES

Index of Subjects and Names

214